Photography: John Lee Studio
Roy Rich, Angel Studio
Christian Delu

Library of Congress Cataloging in Publication Data

Ellis, Audrey.
    Four Seasons cook books.

    Two Continents/Sampson Low.
    Includes indexes.
    CONTENTS: [1] Spring. — [2] Summer. — [3] Autumn.
—[4] Winter.
    1. Cookery. I. Title.
TX652.E38 1976   641.5   75-37432
ISNB 0-8467-0174-X (v. 4)

© Copyright 1975 Purnell & Sons Ltd.
Published 1975 by Sampson Low, Berkshire House,
Queen Street, Maidenhead, Berkshire.
First published in the United States 1976 by
The Two Continents Publishing Group and Sampson Low
30 East 42 Street
New York, N Y 10017
Printed in Italy by
Poligrafici Calderara

Four Seasons Cook Book
Winter

Audrey Ellis

Drawings by Marilyn Day

The Two Continents Publishing Group, Ltd.
Sampson Low

Contents

Useful information

Metric measures: The new standard measure holds 3 dl. (300 ml.) which is just under ½ pint.

1. Sets of metric spoons are available now in the following capacities: — 15 ml. (1 tablespoon), 10 ml., 5 ml. (1 teaspoon), 2.5 ml. The full set comprises two additional spoons, 20 ml. and 1.25 ml. but these are optional. To avoid confusion with earlier standard equipment and existing domestic cutlery, the term 'cup' will be replaced by 'measure' and spoons will eventually be referred to by capacity rather than tablespoon and teaspoon.

2. The new metric measuring jugs contain 1 litre, or ½ litre. The litre jug is marked at 7.5 dl., ½ litre/5 dl., 1.5 dl. and 1 dl.

3. The metric unit of weight is the kilogram (kg.) which is 1000 g. or 2.2 lb. Where recipes give ingredients in ounces, the metric unit of 25 g. has been found practical. Spring balance scales marked in metric or dual-marked in metric and Imperial are available. The pointer shows 1 kilo/2¼ lbs. and indicates divisions of 500 g./18 oz., 250 g./9 oz. and 125 g./4½ oz. Smaller units are marked at intervals of 25 g. Most food packs show weights in both systems, e.g. 4 oz. (113 g.) or 500 g. (1 lb. 1½ oz.).

Oven temperature chart

	°F	°C	Gas Mark
Very cool	225	110	¼
	250	130	½
Cool	275	140	1
	300	150	2
Moderate	325	170	3
	350	180	4
Moderately hot	375	190	5
	400	200	6
Hot	425	220	7
	450	230	8
Very hot	475	240	9

Checking quantities: As personal tastes in seasoning vary, quantities of salt and pepper are left to individual choice unless critical to the success of the recipe. All spoon measures are level. All recipes are to serve 4 unless otherwise indicated.

Seasonal cooking: Many of the recipes given in this book can be used in other seasons. For example there is a summer season for avocados and a winter season. Some items are constantly available frozen or canned.

Acknowledgments

The author and publishers thank the following for their help in supplying photographs for this book
The U.S. Rice Council, p. 17, p. 31.
Farmhouse English Cheddar, p. 18.
Pyrex and Eve 'glass' by James A. Jobling, Ltd., p. 19, p. 78, p. 80.
The White Fish Authority, p. 27.
The New Zealand Lamb Information Bureau, p. 30.
Knorr, p.32, p. 33.
Baxters of Speyside, p. 35.
British Sugar Bureau, p. 36.
The Pasta Information Centre, p. 37.
Gale's Honey, p. 39.
The Carnation Milk Bureau, p. 40.
Tabasco Pepper Sauce, p. 42.
Buxted Brand Products by Ross Poultry, Ltd., p. 44, p. 45.
The British Sausage Bureau, p. 53.
Hassy Perfection Celery, p. 55.
Mazola Pure Corn Oil, p. 58, p. 67.
The Kellogg Company of Great Britain, Ltd., p. 68.
The National Dried Fruit Trade Association, p. 70.
Trex by Princes Foods, Ltd., p. 72.
The National Dairy Council, p. 74.
James Robertson & Sons (Preserve Manufacturers) Ltd., p. 75.
Wall's Ice Cream, p. 76.

Winter comes to rule the varied year

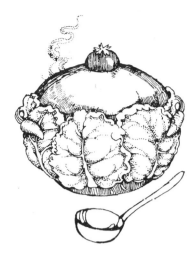

Introduction

Winter days are sometimes delightfully cold and crisp. But just as often they are dark, damp and dreary, making your warm kitchen seem particularly inviting. Get out your biggest casserole dishes. These are days indeed to sample the joys of a New England boiled dinner, or spoil your guests with the wine-rich flavor of Burgundy beef. We may try to forgo hearty stews and puddings in warm weather for diet's sake, but now they make a welcome return to the table.

The season's buying guide reads almost like a page from Dickens. Oranges, pineapples, figs, dates, almonds, brazil nuts enough to overflow the fruit bowl. And the butcher is making a brave show of furred and feathered game, capons and turkeys; even Scrooge's favorite, the traditional goose. Citrus fruits are excellent too, and an orange still makes a good filler for a Christmas stocking. Some time soon, you should get out your canning kettle. Seville oranges are on their way to join lemons, limes, grapefruit and sweet oranges in the shops. January is the month for making marmalade, and, to my mind, bought marmalade cannot compare with the imprisoned sunshine in your own jars.

But Christmas comes first, and its many delights have been catered for in this book. Some can be made in advance and stored: mincemeat, plum puddings, and a minimum-effort cake which can hardly go wrong. I have suggested ways to glaze the cake if you feel no urge to ice it.

My recipes for seasonal meals are divided into groups: simple ones for everyday, and sophisticated ones for entertaining, as indicated below.

Of course, a freezer is your true friend when it comes to advance preparation. Forget the fog and ice, and have a splendid cook-in. Make big, nourishing stews in double portions—one for now and one for the freezer. Start a special Christmas basket or shelf devoted to the festivities. Make up sausages in pastry wraps, mince pies, Brandy and Cumberland butters; even turkey stuffing can be made well beforehand. In a restful moment, draw up a Christmas catering plan and use mine for inspiration. For the adventurous hostess, a pleasant surprise is in store. It is much easier than you think to make marrons glacés, expensive-looking *petits fours*, and glacé fruits for parties. Winter is, above all, the party season; a season when one truly cooks for pleasure, and I hope your pleasure will be increased by the new recipes and ideas you find in this book.

Audrey Ellis

 Sophisticated

 Simple

Buying guide for the season

Storage space is probably at a premium during the Winter months for gardeners. But as you use up your harvest of apples, pears and tomatoes, you should find room for root vegetables which must be removed from the ground before the frost turns it hard as iron. Root vegetables kept in a dark place tend to sprout if the atmosphere is damp, or to shrivel up if it is too dry. For a storage time extending beyond the usual week, pack such vegetables in boxes with layers of sawdust, straw or sand—the old farmhouse way! They should be clean but, if washed, *perfectly dry*, and certainly not peeled since the skin is a natural protection.

In the shops, you can choose between nicely washed imported young carrots, or the larger maincrop carrots which are inevitably coarser and less attractive. Providing the latter have no woody cores, the flavor and tenderness are just as good when cooked, and they are much cheaper. Winter turnips, rutabaga and parsnips are all best after a touch of frost. The only tip on buying is to avoid those with brown spots, spongy patches or holes made by the fork. Do not confuse maincrop turnips with the delicate little early ones available in Spring and early Summer.

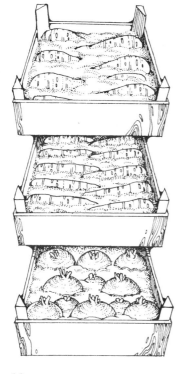

During Winter the small pickling onions of Autumn disappear and the choice is between large mild Spanish onions—though the name now signifies *any* large mild onion—and the maincrop onions which are smaller, with skins varying from straw colour through pale golden brown to a rich bronze. Do not accept any which are soft and spongy around the neck, as the center of the bulb may be uneatable. Other members of the onion family are shallots, much favored on the Continent for their delicate yet slightly garlicky flavor. The best ones have a well-swollen rounded bulb and narrow neck. Garlic itself comes, unlike the cluster of shallots, in a whole bulb. The skin is papery white or pale pink and the bulb is divided into small segments called 'cloves'. Each clove must be separately peeled, and if the bulb has been properly dried and after purchase is kept in a dry, dark place, it will last until all the cloves have been used. The unused cloves tend to wither up eventually.

Jerusalem artichokes, for which I give some recipes, deserve to be better known and more popular, as the flavor is quite unique and delicious. Try to choose large tubers that are even in shape as there is a lot of waste when peeling small or misshapen ones.

Winter cabbages include the firm white cabbage which stores extremely well even when cut. Cover closely, especially the cut surface, with plastic wrap and, providing all air is excluded, a half cabbage may keep for up to a fortnight. The same applies to red cabbages which, when fresh, have a delicate silvery bloom. The round drumhead type with curly leaves has a richer flavor but does not keep so well.

Some of the nuts mentioned in this volume may be strangers to your kitchen. Here is some advice on how to choose for quality.

Chestnuts: Because one is more familiar with canned chestnut purée, which is usually sweetened, the strong flavor of the fresh chestnut can be quite a surprise. The nuts should be bright brown, large and shiny. Dull or wrinkled ones are stale. The nuts are not eaten in the uncooked state, and the shells have to be removed by boiling as many minutes as are necessary to make their removal easy with a sharp, pointed knife. (If you have the oven heated, you can *bake* them until the shells peel off.) Be sure to remove the hard skin or inner shell as well.

The sweet chestnut, which is edible, has a country cousin the horse chestnut, which is inedible; these nuts have a much deeper, reddish-brown color.

Coconuts: Although fresh coconuts are in some supply all year, late fall to winter is definitely their season. The coconut should be heavy for its size and, when shaken, you should be able to hear the milk swish around inside. The outside should be dry, well matted and bright brown in color. If it is damp, the coconut may be moldy, or if there is no milk inside it has dried out and the flesh will be dry in texture. Opening a coconut can be quite a problem. If possible put it in a moderate oven for 15 minutes first; or if this is not convenient, put in the freezer for half an hour. Pierce a couple of 'eyes' with an ice pick to release the vacuum, and drain out the milk. Sounds brutal, but the best way to break it open is to drop it from a height of several feet onto a clean, hard surface, or crack it open with a hammer wrapped in a kitchen towel to keep dirt away from the flesh. Fresh coconut, grated, tastes entirely different from the prepared and packaged kinds, with a nuttier flavor.

Filberts: More often called hazelnuts in Europe, the filbert is actually a cultivated hazelnut. Much of the delicate flavor lies in the skin itself, and as it is less tough than the skin of almonds, it is frequently left on the nut. The shelled nuts can be used ground, chopped or whole with the skins on, or toasted to intensify the flavor. As they are only widely available around Christmas, it is worth keeping some refrigerated and more frozen for long term use.

Mincemeat: This confection is not only made with nuts, but with apple, spices, sugar, shortening and usually cognac. Many years ago it always contained meat (beef, ground lean and fat), and the other ingredients were added as a preservative, but with better storage methods, and changing tastes, it gradually altered to the present form of English mincemeat, which is entirely sweet, and in old recipes, still sometimes called Sweet Mincemeat. English mincemeat is, however, invariably made with raw ground beef suet, in preference to any other fat.

Citrus fruit

Oranges: These are hard to judge for quality by the look of the skins alone as even the best looking ones may be dry, coarse in texture and full of seeds. Bitter oranges, of which the Seville is best, have numerous seeds and acid flesh which makes them unsuitable for the fruit bowl but perfect for making marmalade. Valencia oranges are available from Florida, Arizona or California mostly in summer and the large seedless Navel oranges from the same sources during winter. As all oranges are required by law to be picked mature, color is no indication of ripeness but avoid those that are light in weight as they will lack juice. Blood oranges are round rather than the characteristic oval shape of the Valencias, and include those from Malta, Sicily and Spain—these are usually very fully flavored though more burdened with seeds. Small oranges are usually cheaper, but simply because the proportion of rind and pith to flesh is higher.

Other types of orange with exotic names are best in winter. These include the mandarin, with a loose, light orange skin and many seeds; the tangerine, with a loose almost red skin and many seeds; the clementine, which is more like a genuine orange and has a firm skin. It is practically seedless and so is the satsuma, which has a much paler skin and flesh, the skin sometimes being tinged with green.

Lemons and limes: These can be judged for goodness by their smooth skins and heavy weight for their size. Juicy ones are usually heavy.

Grapefruit: These should be very firm. Again, fruits with a thick spongy peel weigh light in the hand and have a poor content of juice and flesh. Storage for a few days after purchase usually makes them sweet enough to be eaten without sugar. Pink grapefruit with yellow skins and pale pink flesh are particularly sweet.

Unusual fruits of the orange family are crosses between two members. The ugli fruit is a cross between a tangerine and a grapefruit, is larger than the average grapefruit with a very thick slightly greenish skin and occasionally to be seen here in midwinter. The tangelo is, a cross between a tart grapefruit and a sweet tangerine, is about the size of a small grapefruit with dark orange skin which is easy to peel.

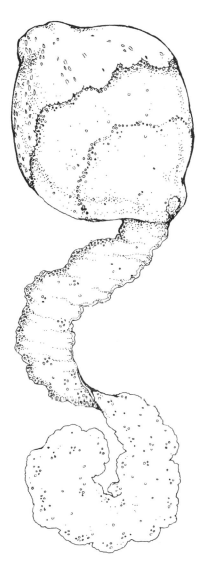

Midwinter — Time to make marmalade

Follow these simple rules for successful marmalade:

1. Choose fruit as fresh as possible. Bitter oranges give a sharp and tangy flavour and are preferable to sweet oranges if you prefer the traditional type marmalade. Any combination of citrus fruits can be used. These include lemons, oranges, grapefruit, tangerines or clementines.

2. Pectin is essential for a well-set marmalade. This is found in the pith (the white layer beneath the peel) and in the seeds. The pith and the seeds must be cooked with the fruit to ensure sufficient pectin for setting.

3. Sugar helps the marmalade set and keep. A general rule is to add 1 lb./450 g. granulated sugar to 1 pint/generous $\frac{1}{2}$ litre juice or pulp.

4. Test for setting after the sugar has been added. Boil the marmalade rapidly and test after 15 minutes, then every five minutes until the setting point is reached. There are three setting tests that can be used. When testing for the setting point, remove the marmalade from the heat so it does not overboil.

    (a) Thermometer — Insert the thermometer in the boiling marmalade, making sure the bulb does not touch the bottom of the saucepan. A reading of 220°F/105°C indicates that setting point is reached.

    (b) Cold plate test — Pour a small amount of marmalade on a cold plate and allow to cool. If a wrinkled skin forms on the surface, the setting point is reached.

    (c) Drop test — Dip a large spoon into the marmalade. Allow the marmalade to run off the spoon. When the setting point is reached the marmalade will partially set on the spoon and drop off the edge of the spoon in one large flake.

5. Storage — Choose jars that are free from chips or cracks, wash well and dry thoroughly in a warm oven. Pour or ladle the marmalade into warm jars placed on a wooden board or newspapers to prevent cracking. Fill the jars to the top as the marmalade will shrink slightly on cooling. Cover the jars with transparent plastic wrap and secure with an elastic band. Store the jars in a cool dry cupboard.

Traditional Seville orange marmalade

Imperial/Metric
3 lb./1½ kg. Seville
  oranges
1 sweet orange
1 lemon
6 pints/3½ litres water
6 lb./3 kg. preserving or
  granulated sugar

American
3 lb. Seville oranges
1 sweet orange
1 lemon
7½ pints water
12 cups sugar

Wash and halve the fruit. Squeeze the juice and scoop out the pulp and the white pith. Strain the juice into a saucepan. Tie the seeds, pulp and pith in a muslin bag. Slice the peel very thinly. Place in the saucepan with the juice, water and muslin bag. Bring to the boil, reduce the heat and cook gently for 2 hours until the peel is soft. Remove the muslin bag and stir in the sugar. Bring to the boil and boil rapidly until the setting point is reached. Skim any foam off the marmalade and leave for 20 minutes. Then pour into warm clean jars and seal.

Makes approximately 10 lb./5 kg.

Three-fruit marmalade

Imperial/Metric
2 grapefruit
4 large sweet oranges
1 lemon
6 pints/3½ litres water
6 lb./3 kg. preserving or
  granulated sugar

American
2 grapefruit
4 large sweet oranges
1 lemon
7½ pints water
12 cups sugar

Wash the fruit well and place in a large pan with the water. Cover and bring to the boil. Cook over low heat for 2 hours or until the fruit pierces easily. Remove the fruit and cool sufficiently to handle. Halve the fruit and remove the seeds. Simmer the seeds in the cooking water for 10 minutes. Strain the liquid and return to the pan. Chop the fruit coarsely and add to the strained liquid. Bring to the boil and stir in the sugar. Boil rapidly until setting point is reached. Skim, leave for 20 minutes, then ladle into jars and seal.

Makes approximately 10 lb./5 kg.

Lemon ginger marmalade

Imperial/Metric
1 oz./25 g. root ginger
2 lb./1 kg. lemons
3 pints/3¾ litres water
2 oz./50 g. stem ginger
3 lb./1½ kg. preserving or
  granulated sugar

American
1 oz. ginger root
2 lb. lemons
7½ cups water
2 oz. preserved ginger
6 cups sugar

Bruise the ginger root with a hammer or weight. Place in a large saucepan with the lemons and water. Bring to the boil, cover and cook gently for 2 hours until the fruit is soft. Remove the fruit and cool sufficiently to handle. Halve the lemons, peel and remove seeds. Simmer the seeds in the cooking liquid for 10 minutes. Strain the liquid and return to the pan. Slice the lemon peel finely and chop the preserved ginger. Add the peel, preserved ginger and pulp to the liquid. Stir in the sugar. Bring to the boil and boil rapidly until the setting point is reached. Skim, let cool for 20 minutes, ladle into jars and seal.

Makes approximately 5 lb./2½ kg.

Tangerine and grapefruit marmalade

Imperial/Metric
1½ lb./¾ kg. tangerine
½ pint/3 dl. water
2 grapefruit
1 lemon
4½ pints/2½ litres water
2 teaspoons tartaric acid
3 lb./1½ kg. preserving or
   granulated sugar

American
1½ lb. tangerines
1¼ cups water
2 grapefruit
1 lemon
11¼ cups water
2 teaspoons cream of tartar
6 cups sugar

Remove the peel from 3 tangerines and shred finely. Place the shredded peel in a saucepan with ½ pint/3 dl. water. Bring to the boil, cover, and cook gently for 30 minutes until the peel is soft. Set aside. Cut the grapefruits, lemon, tangerine pulp and remaining tangerines into small pieces. Place in a large saucepan with the 4½ pints/2½ litres water and the cream of tartar. Bring to the boil, cover and cook gently for 2 hours until the fruit is soft. Pour the pulp into a jelly bag and allow the juice to drip overnight. The next day, strain the juice into a large saucepan. Stir in the sugar and the reserved peel and liquid. Bring to the boil and boil rapidly until setting point is reached. Remove from the heat and skim. Cool 20 minutes, ladle into jars and seal.

Makes approximately 5 lb./2½ kg.

Orange jelly marmalade

Imperial/Metric
2 lb./1 kg. Seville oranges
2 lemons
5 pints/3 litres water
3 lb./1½ kg. preserving or
   granulated sugar approx.

American
2 lb. Seville oranges
2 lemons
6¼ pints water
6 cups sugar approx.

Chop the oranges and lemons coarsely. Place in a large saucepan and cover with the water. Bring to the boil, cover and simmer for 2 hours until the fruit is tender. Pour the fruit into a muslin jelly bag and allow the juice to drip overnight into a container. Measure the juice and allow 1 lb /450 g sugar to 1 pint/generous ½ litre juice. Stir the juice and sugar over low heat until the sugar dissolves. Then boil rapidly until setting point is reached. Skim off any foam, leave for 20 minutes, then pour into jars and seal.

Makes approximately 5 lb./2½ kg.

Lime jelly marmalade

Imperial/Metric
1 lb./450 g. fresh limes
1 lemon
2½ pints/1½ litres water
2 lb./1 kg. preserving or
   granulated sugar

American
1 lb. fresh limes
1 lemon
6¼ cups water
4 cups sugar

Chop the limes and lemon coarsely. Place in a large saucepan and add the water. Bring to the boil, cover and cook gently until the fruit is soft. Pour the fruit into a jelly bag and allow the juice to drip overnight. Do not squeeze the jelly bag. The next day, add the sugar to the juice and bring to the boil. Boil rapidly until the setting point is reached. Skim off any foam, leave for 20 minutes, then pour into jars and seal.

Makes approximately 3 lb./1½ kg.

Starters

Hot soups and even small hot savories make an acceptable first course for winter meals. Miniature soufflés are delicious if you can time them correctly. Wait until your guests arrive, fold in the egg whites and pop them in the oven while the sherry is being consumed. If the main dish is meat or game, a fish soup makes the menu reasonably substantial without the complications of serving four courses.

Winter vegetable minestra

Imperial/Metric
1 medium carrot
1 large onion
1 small parsnip
1 small turnip
2 tablespoons oil
1 pint/generous ½ litre beef stock
1 bay leaf
½ teaspoon salt
¼ teaspoon pepper
1 small potato
8 oz./227 g. can tomatoes
1 teaspoon dried parsley
1 oz./25 g. Vermicelli or noodles
Parmesan cheese

American
1 medium carrot
1 large onion
1 small parsnip
1 small turnip
2 tablespoons oil
2½ cups beef broth
1 bay leaf
½ teaspoon salt
¼ teaspoon pepper
1 small potato
1 cup canned tomatoes
1 teaspoon dried parsley
¼ cup Vermicelli or noodles
Parmesan cheese

Peel and cut the carrot, onion, parsnip and turnip into narrow strips. Heat the oil in a saucepan and fry the vegetables until limp, about 5 minutes. Add the beef stock, bay leaf, salt and pepper. Simmer for 30 minutes. Peel and cut the potato into narrow strips. Add potato strips to the vegetable-stock mixture and simmer for a further 20 minutes. Stir in the tomatoes, parsley and Vermicelli. Simmer 10 minutes, pour into hot soup bowls and sprinkle with grated Parmesan cheese.

Jerusalem soup

Imperial/Metric
1 lb./½ kg. Jerusalem artichokes
1 medium onion
1 oz./25 g. butter
2 tablespoons flour
8 oz./227 g. can tomatoes
1 pint/generous ½ litre chicken stock
1 strip of orange rind
pinch ground mace
salt and pepper
2 fl. oz./50 ml. orange juice
grated orange zest

American
1 lb. Jerusalem artichokes
1 medium onion
2 tablespoons butter or margarine
2 tablespoons all-purpose flour
1 cup canned tomatoes
2½ cups chicken broth
1 strip of orange rind
dash ground mace
salt and pepper
¼ cup orange juice
grated orange rind

Peel and slice the artichokes and onion. Sauté the sliced artichokes and onion in the butter until softened. Stir in the flour. Add the tomatoes, chicken stock, orange rind and seasonings. Cover and simmer for 15 minutes. Remove the orange rind. Liquidize the soup in a blender or rub it through a sieve. Pour into a clean saucepan. Add the orange juice and reheat gently. Garnish with the grated orange rind.

Chinese style rice soup

Imperial/Metric
1 tablespoon oil
4 oz./125 g. long grain rice
3 pints/1½ litres chicken stock
1 carrot
1 leek, trimmed
2 sticks celery
salt and pepper

American
1 tablespoon oil
½ cup long grain rice
4 pints chicken broth
1 carrot
1 leek, trimmed
2 stalks celery
salt and pepper

Heat the oil, use to fry the rice for a few minutes, until transparent. Add the stock, bring to the boil and simmer for 30 minutes. Meanwhile finely chop the carrot, leek and celery. Add the chopped vegetables, simmer for a further 5 minutes, and adjust the seasoning. Serves 6.

Cheddar cheese soup

Imperial/Metric
3 tablespoons grated onion
3 tablespoons grated carrot
1½ oz./40 g. butter
2 pts./generous 1 litre
  chicken stock
½ teaspoon dry mustard
½ teaspoon paprika pepper
¼ pt./1½ dl. milk
2 tablespoons cornflour
4 oz./125 g. Cheddar
  cheese, grated
salt and pepper to taste
2 tablespoons chopped
  parsley

American
3 tablespoons grated onion
3 tablespoons grated carrot
3 tablespoons butter
5 cups chicken broth
½ teaspoon dry mustard
½ teaspoon paprika
½ cup milk
2 tablespoons cornstarch
1 cup grated Cheddar
  cheese
salt and pepper to taste
2 tablespoons chopped
  parsley

Sauté the onion and carrot in the butter over low heat for 10 minutes. Add the chicken stock, mustard, and paprika, and simmer for 15 minutes. Combine the milk and cornstarch. Add to the pan and cook, stirring constantly until mixture thickens. Simmer for 4 minutes. Add the cheese and stir until it is melted. Season to taste and serve garnished with parsley. Serves 6.

Artichoke and green pea soup

Imperial/Metric
2 lb./1 kg. Jerusalem
  artichokes
1 lb./450 g. potatoes
4 oz./125 g. frozen peas
1½-2 pints/scant 1 litre—
  generous 1 litre
  chicken stock
salt and pepper
grated nutmeg
4-5 tablespoons cream
chopped parsley

American
2 lb. Jerusalem artichokes
1 lb. potatoes
1 cup frozen peas
4-5 cups chicken broth
salt and pepper
grated nutmeg
4-5 tablespoons cream
chopped parsley

Scrub the artichokes and potatoes and drop them into a large pan of boiling salted water. Bring back to the boil and simmer for 15-20 minutes, or until vegetables are tender. Cook the peas in a little boiling salted water. Drain artichokes and potatoes and peel as soon as they are cool enough to handle. Rub the artichokes, potatoes and peas through a sieve or blend and return to the rinsed out pan. Add chicken stock to artichoke purée gradually, stirring with a wooden spoon until desired consistency is reached, and reheat gently until soup comes to boiling point, stirring occasionally. Remove pan from heat. Season to taste with salt, pepper and nutmeg. Lightly whip the cream and swirl over the top of the soup. Garnish with parsley. Serves 6.

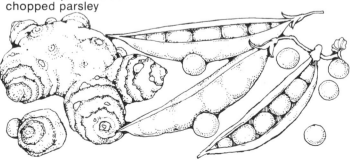

Saffron fish soup

Imperial/Metric
1 head fennel
3 medium onions
1 clove garlic
2 tablespoons oil
salt and pepper
1 bay leaf
$\frac{1}{2}$ teaspoon dried thyme
$\frac{1}{4}$ pint/1$\frac{1}{2}$ dl. white wine
1$\frac{1}{2}$ lbs./$\frac{3}{4}$ kg. cod fillet
1 pint/$\frac{1}{2}$ litre water
pinch powdered saffron
large strip orange rind

American
1 head fennel
3 medium onions
1 clove garlic
2 tablespoons oil
salt and pepper
1 bay leaf
$\frac{1}{2}$ teaspoon dried thyme
$\frac{1}{2}$ cup white wine
1$\frac{1}{2}$ lb. cod fillets
2$\frac{1}{2}$ cups water
dash powdered saffron
large strip orange rind

Trim and finely chop the fennel, onions and garlic and sauté in the oil until softened but not browned. Season with salt and pepper, and add the bay leaf, thyme and wine. Skin the fish, cut into chunks and add to the pan with the water, saffron and orange rind. Cook over gentle heat covered for 45 minutes. Remove orange rind and bay leaf and serve hot with toast.

Fennel and almond fish soup

Imperial/Metric
8 oz./225 g. plaice fillets
1 medium onion
4 peppercorns
1 tablespoon fennel seeds
2 fl. oz./50 ml. dry white wine
2 oz./50 g. blanched almonds
2 fl. oz./50 ml. soured cream
chopped fresh dill

American
$\frac{1}{2}$ lb. flounder fillets
1 medium onion
4 peppercorns
1 tablespoon fennel seeds
$\frac{1}{4}$ cup dry white wine
$\frac{1}{3}$ cup blanched almonds
$\frac{1}{4}$ cup sour cream
chopped fresh dill

Remove the skin from the fish fillets and slice the onion. Poach the fillets, onion, peppercorns, fennel seeds, in the white wine and enough water to cover them. When the fish flakes easily, remove it from the poaching liquid. Place the fish and almonds in a blender with the strained cooking liquid. Blend until smooth. Strain to remove any fine bones. Return to a clean saucepan and reheat. Stir in the sour cream. Pour into hot soup bowls. Sprinkle generously with freshly chopped dill.

Herring potato balls with dill

Imperial/Metric
1 lb./450 g. potatoes
1 egg
1 teaspoon dill seed
salt and pepper
8 oz./225 g. cooked herring
dry breadcrumbs
oil for frying

American
1 lb. potatoes
1 egg
1 teaspoon dill seed
salt and pepper
$\frac{1}{2}$ lb. cooked herring
dry bread crumbs
oil for frying

Cook the potatoes in boiling salted water until tender. Mash, then beat in the egg, dill seed, salt and pepper. Cut the cooked herring into 24 small pieces. Shape the mashed potatoes into small balls, pressing a piece of herring into the middle of each ball. Roll the potato balls in dry breadcrumbs. Fry in hot deep oil until lightly browned. Drain and spear on cocktail sticks. Serve hot.

Drained sardines may be substituted for the herring.

☆ Melon cocktails

Imperial/Metric
1 small Ogen melon
8 oz./225 g. lychees
4 pieces stem ginger
2 tablespoons ginger syrup

American
1 small canteloupe
1 cup lychees
4 pieces preserved ginger
2 tablespoons ginger syrup

Cut the melon in half, remove seeds and scoop out flesh with a melon baller. Reserve the juices. Peel the lychees and slice the stem ginger. Mix together the melon juice with the ginger syrup. Divide the fruit between four small glass dishes, pour over the syrup and decorate with the sliced ginger.

☆ Grilled grapefruit with brown sugar

Imperial/Metric
2 pink grapefruit
4 tablespoons soft brown
  sugar
1 tablespoon rum

American
2 pink grapefruit
4 tablespoons light brown
  sugar
1 tablespoon rum

Cut the grapefruit in half and remove white pith from centers. Loosen segments if necessary. Mix the sugar with the rum, fill centers and spread partly over the surface of the cut halves. Place under a moderately hot grill for a few minutes until sugar melts and caramelizes. Serve hot.

★ Cauliflower and bacon ramekins

Imperial/Metric
1 small cauliflower
$\frac{1}{4}$ pint/1$\frac{1}{2}$ dl. milk
$\frac{3}{4}$ oz./20 g. butter
$\frac{1}{2}$ oz./15 g. flour
salt and pepper
$\frac{1}{4}$ teaspoon grated nutmeg
4 tablespoons cooked
  macaroni
2 oz./50g. streaky bacon
2 tablespoons single cream
2 oz./50 g. Cheddar cheese,
  grated

American
1 small cauliflower
$\frac{1}{2}$ cup milk
1$\frac{1}{2}$ tablespoons butter
2 tablespoons all-purpose
  flour
salt and pepper
$\frac{1}{4}$ teaspoon grated nutmeg
4 tablespoons cooked
  macaroni
2 slices bacon
2 tablespoons coffee cream
$\frac{1}{2}$ cup grated Cheddar
  cheese

Break the cauliflower into florets and cook in boiling salted water for about 10 minutes, or until just tender. Drain, and add the water to the milk to make 8 fl. oz./225 ml. Melt the butter, stir in the flour, cook for 1 minute, add the milk liquid, salt, pepper and nutmeg and cook, stirring constantly, over a moderate heat until smooth and thick. Divide the cooked macaroni among four greased individual ovenproof casseroles. Dice the bacon finely, and fry lightly. Mix the bacon bits with the cauliflower florets and place on top of the macaroni. Pour over the sauce, then a little cream and finally sprinkle with grated cheese. Place under a hot grill until the surface is crisp and golden.

 # Little soufflés

Imperial/Metric
2 oz./50 g. Lancashire
   cheese
3 oz./75 g. blue Stilton
2 oz./50 g. butter
1 oz./25 g. flour
4 eggs, separated
8 fl. oz./225 ml. milk
1 slice white bread

American
2 oz. American cheese
3 oz. blue Stilton
¼ cup butter
¼ cup all-purpose flour
4 eggs, separated
1 cup milk
1 slice white bread

Crumble the cheeses and beat together with 1½ oz./40 g. of the butter, the flour and yolks of the eggs. Stir in the milk and finally fold in the stiffly beaten egg whites. Toast the bread lightly, spread with remaining butter, divide into four and place the pieces in the bottoms of four well buttered ramekin dishes. Divide the soufflé mixture among the dishes and cook in a moderately hot oven (375°F, 190°C, Gas Mark 5) for about 20 minutes until well risen and golden brown on top. Serve immediately.
Note: The soufflé mixture can be prepared in advance up to the stage of folding in the beaten egg whites.

Avocado starters

Imperial/Metric	American
2 avocado pears	2 avocados
1 canned red pimiento	1 canned red pimiento
1 large carrot	1 large carrot
4 oz./125 g. Webb's lettuce	½ small Bibb lettuce
8 canned anchovy fillets	8 canned anchovy fillets
2 tablespoons mayonnaise	2 tablespoons mayonnaise

Cut the avocados in half and remove the stones. Slice the pimiento finely, coarsely grate the carrot and shred the lettuce. Reserve 4 anchovy fillets and 4 pieces of red pimiento for the garnish. Chop the remaining anchovy fillets roughly, toss together with the sliced pimiento, the carrot, lettuce and mayonnaise. Divide the filling between the four portions, topping each one with an anchovy fillet rolled round a piece of pimiento. If liked, serve with lettuce leaves as the stuffed avocado is rather rich.

Turkey appetiser wedges

Imperial/Metric	American
4 oz./125 g. cooked turkey	½ cup cooked turkey
3 oz./85 g. cream cheese	3 oz. package cream cheese
2 oz./50 g. finely chopped almonds	¼ cup finely chopped almonds
2 oz./50 g. salad cream	¼ cup salad dressing
1 teaspoon lemon juice	1 teaspoon lemon juice
2 tablespoons cranberry sauce	2 tablespoons cranberry sauce
salt and pepper	salt and pepper
finely chopped parsley	finely chopped parsley

Finely chop the cooked turkey. Thoroughly mix together the first six ingredients. Season to taste with salt and pepper. Chill for several hours. Form the turkey mixture into a ball. Flatten and roll the ball in the chopped parsley. Serve cut in wedges with assorted biscuits or crackers.

Pheasant pâté

Imperial/Metric	American
1 oz./25 g. butter	2 tablespoons butter
4 oz./100 g. calves liver	¼ lb. calf liver
1 lb./450 g. cooked pheasant	2 cups cooked pheasant
4 oz./100 g. ham	¼ lb. ham
1 onion	1 onion
salt and freshly ground black pepper	salt and freshly ground black pepper
pinch dried thyme	dash dried thyme
1 tablespoon chopped parsley	1 tablespoon chopped parsley
1-2 tablespoons brandy	1-2 tablespoons brandy
1 egg	1 egg
6 oz./175 g. streaky bacon thinly sliced	9 thin bacon slices

Heat the butter in a frying pan and quickly sauté the calves liver. Put the game, ham, onion and liver through the finest blade of a meat grinder. Add the salt, pepper, thyme, parsley, brandy and beaten egg. Blend the mixture thoroughly. Stretch the bacon slices with the back of a knife. Use two-thirds of them to line a 1½-pint/1 litre foil dish, earthenware dish or loaf tin. Pack the pâté mixture into the bacon-lined dish and place the remaining bacon over the surface. Cover securely with foil or a lid. Stand the dish in a roasting pan and pour water into the pan to come half way up the sides of the dish. Cook in the center of a moderate oven (350°F, 180°C, Gas Mark 4) for 1½ hours. Leave the pâté in the container, under a heavy weight, to cool.

Main dishes

On a frosty winter's day, everyone enjoys a hearty dish, piping hot. Firm white fish is in good supply, and a simple fish pie is a positive treat. Beef is delicious, and with the turn of the year, look out for new arrivals, Australian and New Zealand lamb. Turkey is a mid-winter 'must' for Christmas, and made-up dishes for the leftovers will serve equally well for chicken.

Curried fish kedgeree

Imperial/Metric
12 oz./350 g. cod fillet
8 oz./225 g. smoked cod fillet
1 tablespoon oil
2 oz./50 g. butter
1 large onion, chopped
4 oz./125 g. long grain rice
1 tablespoon curry powder
1 teaspoon salt
5 oz./150 g. can red pimientoes
3 sprigs parsley to garnish

American
$\frac{3}{4}$ lb. cod fillet
$\frac{1}{2}$ lb. smoked cod fillet
1 tablespoon oil
$\frac{1}{4}$ cup butter
1 large onion, chopped
generous $\frac{1}{2}$ cup long grain rice
1 tablespoon curry powder
1 teaspoon salt
5 oz. can pimientoes
3 sprigs parsley to garnish

Poach the white and smoked fish in gently boiling water until just tender. Drain, and flake. Heat the oil and butter and use to sauté the onion until pale golden, stir in the rice, curry powder and salt and cook, stirring, for 2 minutes. Add $\frac{1}{2}$ pint/3 dl./$1\frac{1}{4}$ cups boiling water, cover and cook until all the water is absorbed. Chop the pimiento, reserving the liquor. Add this to the rice mixture if it becomes too dry. Stir the pimiento into it with the flaked fish and heat through. Transfer to a warm serving dish and garnish with parsley.

Halibut with carnival topping

Imperial/Metric
1 tablespoon lemon juice
3 small halibut steaks
salt and pepper
1 medium onion
1 large tomato
2 tablespoons oil
2 tablespoons chopped
  green pepper

American
1 tablespoon lemon juice
3 small halibut steaks
salt and pepper
1 medium onion
1 large tomato
2 tablespoons oil
2 tablespoons chopped
  green pepper

Mix the lemon juice with just sufficient water to make a poaching stock for the halibut steaks. Season fish lightly with salt and pepper, place in a shallow oven-proof dish, pour the stock round and cover with foil. Place in a moderate oven (350°F, 180°C, Gas Mark 4) for about 15 minutes, or until fish parts easily from the bone when tested with a fork. Meanwhile finely chop the onion and peel and remove seeds from the tomato. Cook the onion in the oil until just limp but not colored. Add the green pepper, cook for a further 3 minutes, then add the chopped tomato. Cook, stirring gently, until well blended and heated through. Drain off stock from fish if necessary using paper towels. Spoon the carnival topping over the fish and serve hot. Serves 3.

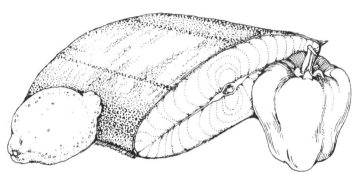

Fish pie with rutabaga purée

Imperial/Metric
1 lb./450 g. cooked potato
salt and pepper
little milk
1 lb./450 g. cod fillet
4 oz./125 g. frozen peas
cheese sauce:
1 pint/generous $\frac{1}{2}$ litre milk
1 oz./25 g. butter
$\frac{3}{4}$ oz./20 g. flour
4 oz./125 g. Cheddar
   cheese, grated
swede purée:
1 large or 2 medium swedes
1 oz./25 g. butter
$\frac{1}{2}$ teaspoon grated nutmeg
salt and pepper
1 tablespoon chopped
   parsley

American
1 lb. cooked potato
salt and pepper
little milk
1 lb. cod fillet
1 cup frozen peas
cheese sauce:
$2\frac{1}{2}$ cups milk
2 tablespoons butter
3 tablespoons all-purpose
   flour
1 cup grated Cheddar
   cheese
rutabaga purée:
1 large or 2 medium
   rutabagas
2 tablespoons butter
$\frac{1}{2}$ teaspoon grated nutmeg
salt and pepper
1 tablespoon chopped
   parsley

Mash the potato in the saucepan in which it was cooked, with seasoning to taste and sufficient milk to give a firm consistency for forcing through a pastry bag. Keep hot. Poach the fish in the milk for the sauce and add seasoning to taste. Remove fish and flake roughly. To make the sauce, melt the butter in a saucepan and stir in the flour. Cook for 1 minute, stirring. Gradually add the strained milk from cooking the fish and bring to the boil, stirring constantly, until the sauce is smooth and thickened. Add the peas and grated cheese and re-heat until bubbling. Lightly fold in the flaked fish and pour the mixture into a warm ovenproof glass dish. Place the warm potato in a pastry bag fitted with a large star nozzle. Make large potato rosettes on the fish mixture to come well above the edge of the dish. Place under a moderately hot grill for a few minutes until the surface turns golden brown. Meanwhile, peel, chop and cook the rutabaga until tender in boiling salted water. Drain well and mash with half the butter, the nutmeg, salt and pepper to taste. Turn purée into a warm serving dish, place the remaining butter in the center and sprinkle with parsley.

Scallop mélange au gratin

Imperial/Metric
4 large scallops
½ pint/3 dl. water
¼ pint/1½ dl. dry white wine
slice of onion
1 bay leaf
½ teaspoon salt
2 peppercorns
1 medium carrot, peeled
1 stick celery
4 large Brussels sprouts
2 tablespoons butter
salt and pepper
sauce:
1 tablespoon butter
1 tablespoon flour
¼ pint/1½ dl. milk
1 oz./25 g. Cheddar cheese, grated
salt and pepper
paprika pepper

American
4 scallops
1¼ cups water
½ cup dry white wine
slice of onion
1 bay leaf
½ teaspoon salt
2 peppercorns
1 medium carrot, peeled
1 stalk celery
4 large Brussels sprouts
2 tablespoons butter or margarine
salt and pepper
sauce:
1 tablespoon butter
1 tablespoon all-purpose flour
⅔ cup milk
¼ cup grated Cheddar cheese
salt and pepper
paprika

Clean the scallops. Combine the water, white wine, onion, bay leaf, salt and peppercorns, in a small saucepan. Add the scallops, bring to the boil and simmer for 5 minutes. Finely dice the carrot and celery. Wash and slice the Brussels sprouts. Sauté the vegetables in the butter until soft. Season with salt and pepper. Place a small amount of the vegetables in individual ovenproof dishes or scallop shells. Drain and slice the scallops. Arrange on top of the vegetables. Make a cheese sauce by melting the butter in a small saucepan. Stir in the flour, gradually add the milk and cook until thickened, stirring constantly. Add the grated cheese. Season to taste with salt and pepper. Pour over the scallop and vegetable mixture. Dust generously with paprika and brown under a hot grill.

Spanish-style fish

Imperial/Metric
1 medium onion
1 clove garlic
4 tomatoes
1 tablespoon olive oil
1 oz./25 g. chopped walnuts
2 teaspoons grated orange zest
2 tablespoons orange juice
4 fl. oz./125 ml. dry white wine
4 portions cod, haddock or turbot
salt and pepper
orange slices to garnish

American
1 medium onion
1 clove garlic
4 tomatoes
1 tablespoon olive oil
¼ cup chopped walnuts
2 teaspoons grated orange rind
2 tablespoons orange juice
½ cup dry white wine
4 portions white-fleshed fish
salt and pepper
orange slices to garnish

Chop the onion and crush the garlic. Peel, seed and chop the tomatoes. Fry the onion and garlic in the olive oil until soft. Stir in the chopped tomato, walnuts, orange rind and juice and the white wine. Bring to simmering point, then add the fish portions. Simmer gently until tender. Arrange the cooked fish on a warm serving platter. Season the sauce with salt and pepper and pour over the fish. Garnish with orange slices.

Fillet of sole with mustard sauce

Imperial/Metric
8 sole fillets
2 tablespoons mild continental mustard
salt and pepper
¼ pint/1½ dl. water
¼ pint/1½ dl. dry white wine
1 tablespoon chopped parsley or
1 teaspoon dried parsley
½ oz./15 g. butter
¼ pint/1½ dl. double cream
salt and pepper

American
8 sole fillets
2 tablespoons mild mustard
salt and pepper
½ cup water
½ cup dry white wine
1 tablespoon chopped parsley or
1 teaspoon dried parsley
1 tablespoon butter
½ cup whipping cream
salt and pepper

Spread a little of the mustard on one side of the skinned and boned sole fillets. Season with salt and pepper, then roll up each fillet with the mustard on the inside. Stand the rolls upright in a buttered baking dish. Pour the water and wine around the fillets: sprinkle with the parsley and dot with butter. Bake in a moderate oven (350°F, 180°C, Gas Mark 4) for 20 minutes. Arrange the fillets on a warm serving platter. Reduce the cooking liquid to half by fast boiling, then stir in the remaining mustard and the cream. Season to taste with salt and pepper. Pour the mustard sauce over the fillet rolls.

 # Colonial goose

Imperial/Metric
$4\frac{1}{2}$ lb./$2\frac{1}{4}$ kg. leg lamb
4 oz./125 g. dried apricots
4 oz./125 g. fresh white
  breadcrumbs
1 oz./25 g. butter
1 tablespoon clear honey
2 oz./50 g. grated onion
$\frac{1}{4}$ teaspoon dried thyme
$\frac{1}{4}$ teaspoon salt
pinch freshly ground black
  pepper
1 egg

American
$4\frac{1}{2}$ lb. leg lamb
scant $\frac{3}{4}$ cup dried apricots
2 cups fresh white bread
  crumbs
2 tablespoons butter
1 tablespoon clear honey
$\frac{1}{4}$ cup minced onion
$\frac{1}{4}$ teaspoon dried thyme
$\frac{1}{4}$ teaspoon salt
dash freshly ground black
  pepper
1 egg

Lay the meat, fat side down, on a wooden board. With a small, sharp pointed knife, work the meat away from the bone, from the top of the leg down to the first joint. Now, cut along the line of the bone from the opposite end of the leg. Work the flesh away from the bone, being careful not to puncture the skin in any other place. Sever the bone from all the flesh and ligaments and draw out the bone. With a pair of scissors, snip the apricots in two. Place the breadcrumbs in a bowl and stir in the apricots. Put the butter into a small saucepan and add honey. Stir over low heat until melted, then stir in the onion. Add to the breadcrumb mixture, with the herbs and seasoning. Beat the egg lightly, pour into stuffing ingredients and beat until well blended. Stuff the leg and weigh it. Roast in a moderate oven, (350°F, 180°C, Gas Mark 4) for $2\frac{1}{4}$-$2\frac{1}{2}$ hours. Serves 8.

Minced meat rolls with Palma salad

Imperial/Metric
2 large mild onions
6 oz./150 g. cooked long
  grain rice
8 oz./250 g. minced beef
1 tablespoon capers
salt and pepper
1 teaspoon made mustard
½ teaspoon grated lemon
  zest
1 egg, beaten
3 tablespoons corn oil
2 medium tomatoes
1 teaspoon wine vinegar
paprika pepper
celery salt

American
2 large mild onions
1½ cups cooked long grain
  rice
½ lb. ground beef
1 tablespoon capers
salt and pepper
1 teaspoon prepared
  mustard
½ teaspoon grated lemon
  rind
1 egg, beaten
3 tablespoons corn oil
2 medium tomatoes
1 teaspoon wine vinegar
paprika
celery salt

Chop one of the onions finely and mix with the rice and ground beef, then blend in the capers, seasonings, mustard and lemon rind. Bind the mixture with beaten egg and form into long rolls with floured hands. Fry the rolls in 2 tablespoons of the oil until crisp and browned on all sides. Meanwhile slice the tomatoes and remaining onion finely, season with salt. Mix together the remaining oil and the vinegar with the paprika and celery salt. Pour over the tomatoes. Toss with the onion rings. Serve the salad with the hot meat rolls.

31

Boiled dinner New England style

Imperial/Metric
1 lb./450 g. piece brisket
  of beef
3½ lb./1¾ kg. roasting
  chicken
1 chicken stock cube
1 beef stock cube
½ teaspoon dried mixed
  herbs
¼ teaspoon ground mixed
  spices
1 lb./450 g. carrots
1 small savoy cabbage
1 small swede
1 lb./450 g. medium onions
salt and pepper.

American
1 lb. boneless beef
  brisket
3½ lb. roasting chicken
1 chicken bouillon cube
1 beef bouillon cube
½ teaspoon dried mixed
  herbs
¼ teaspoon ground mixed
  spice
1 lb. carrots
1 small savoy cabbage
1 small rutabaga
1 lb. medium onions
salt and pepper

Put the trimmed beef with the chicken in a deep oval casserole with the bouillon cubes, herbs and spices. Cover with water to half the depth of the chicken, cover and simmer for 30 minutes. Quarter the carrots and cabbage and cut the rutabaga into chunks. Add the carrots, onions and rutabaga to the casserole, cover and cook for 40 minutes. Add the cabbage and cook for a further 20 minutes. Adjust seasoning. Serves 6.

Golden potato-topped pie with onions

Imperial/Metric
2 beef stock cubes
1 lb./450 g. minced cooked
  or raw lamb or beef
3 tablespoons corn oil
8 oz./225 g. finely chopped
  swede
1 teaspoon mixed sweet
  herbs
1 tablespoon tomato purée
2 teaspoons brown sugar
1 tablespoon flour
salt and pepper
1 lb./450 g. potatoes, diced
¼ pint/1½ dl. milk
1 egg
4 medium onions

American
2 beef bouillon cubes
1 lb. ground cooked
  or raw lamb or beef
3 tablespoons corn oil
1½ cups finely chopped
  rutabaga
1 teaspoon mixed sweet
  herbs
1 tablespoon tomato paste
2 teaspoons brown sugar
1 tablespoon flour
salt and pepper
2 cups diced potato
⅔ cup milk
1 egg
4 medium onions

Dissolve the bouillon cubes in 1 pint/½ litre/2½ cups boiling water. Sauté the meat in 2 tablespoons hot oil, stirring frequently, for 2 minutes. Add the rutabaga, herbs, tomato purée, sugar, and finally the flour. Pour in half the stock and stir until thick over moderate heat. Taste and adjust seasoning. Cook the potatoes in boiling salted water, drain, mash with the milk, season well and beat in the egg. At the same time parboil the onions in the remaining stock. Turn the meat mixture into a greased ovenproof dish, spread the mashed potato on top and score the surface with a fork. Arrange the onions in a small baking dish, mix the remaining corn oil with the rest of the stock and pour over them. Place both dishes in a hot oven (425°F, 220°C, Gas Mark 7) for 20 minutes, until golden.

Stuffed cabbage rolls

Imperial/Metric
4 large leaves Savoy
   cabbage
1½ oz./40 g. butter
8 oz./225 g. minced beef
1 small onion, chopped
salt and pepper
6 oz./175 g. fresh white
   breadcrumbs
good pinch grated nutmeg
½ teaspoon dried marjoram
1 oz./25 g. grated
   Parmesan cheese
1 egg
2 tablespoons oil
1 beef stock cube
½ pint/3 dl. water
8 oz./225 g. mashed potato

American
4 large leaves Savoy
   cabbage
3 tablespoons butter
½ lb. ground beef
1 small onion, chopped
salt and pepper
2 cups fresh white bread
   crumbs
good dash grated nutmeg
½ teaspoon dried marjoram
¼ cup grated Parmesan
   cheese
1 egg
2 tablespoons oil
1 beef bouillon cube
1¼ cups water
2 cups mashed potato

Trim the hard stems from the base of the cabbage leaves and blanch in boiling salted water for about 10 minutes, or until tender. Melt ½ oz./15 g. of the butter and use to sauté the beef and onion until lightly browned. Season with salt and pepper. Combine with the breadcrumbs, nutmeg, marjoram, Parmesan and the lightly beaten egg. Divide the stuffing between the cabbage leaves and roll each up into a parcel. Tie a piece of thread round the center of each parcel, following the spine of the leaf. Brown the rolls on all sides in the remaining butter and the oil in a shallow flameproof dish. Dissolve the bouillon cube in the water, pour over, and braise, covered, for 45 minutes, over low heat. Remove the thread, place the rolls on a serving dish, reduce remaining stock to a few spoonfuls and pour over the rolls. Serve garnished with rosettes of mashed potato.

☆ Royal liver casserole

Imperial/Metric
1 lb./450 g. ox liver
1 oz./25 g. plain flour
oil for frying
1 large onion
1 large green pepper
salt and pepper
1 tablespoon tomato purée
1 can Royal Game Soup

American
1 lb. beef liver
¼ cup all-purpose flour
oil for frying
1 large onion
1 large green pepper
salt and pepper
1 tablespoon tomato paste
1 can game soup

Slice the liver and coat with plain flour. Brown on both sides in a little hot oil and put on one side. Slice the onion and seed and slice the green pepper. Fry these gently until soft and season well with salt and pepper. Place liver and vegetables in an ovenproof casserole. Blend tomato paste with the soup and pour over. Cover and bake in a moderate oven (350°F, 180°C, Gas Mark 4) for 1½-2 hours until the liver is tender. Alternatively, simmer gently on top of the range for 1¼ hours. Serve with fluffy boiled rice.

Burgundy beef

Imperial/Metric
1½ lb./¾ kg. braising steak
1 tablespoon olive oil
1 oz./25 g. butter
1 medium onion
1 clove garlic
1 oz./25 g. plain flour
1 beef stock cube
½ pint/3 dl. boiling water
1 tablespoon soft brown
  sugar
8 oz./227 g. can tomatoes
1 teaspoon tomato purée
½ pint/3 dl. full bodied
  red wine
4 oz./125 g. mushrooms,
  sliced
salt and pepper.

American
1½ lb. round steak
1 tablespoon olive oil
2 tablespoons butter
1 medium onion
1 clove garlic
¼ cup all-purpose flour
1 beef bouillon cube
1¼ cups boiling water
1 tablespoon light brown
  sugar
1 cup canned tomatoes
1 teaspoon tomato paste
1¼ cups full bodied red
  wine
1 cup sliced mushrooms
salt and pepper

Remove any excess fat from the steak and cut it into 2 inch/5 cm. squares. Heat the oil and butter in a large saucepan and use to fry the meat until browned. Remove meat from the pan and add the finely chopped onion and garlic. Cook until beginning to brown. Add the flour and cook for about 1 minute. Gradually add the bouillon cube dissolved in the water and bring to the boil, stirring constantly. Add the sugar, tomatoes, tomato paste and the wine. Return the meat to the saucepan and bring to the boil again, stirring. Cover and simmer for 1 hour. Add the mushrooms and seasoning to taste and simmer for a further 15 minutes, or until the meat is tender.

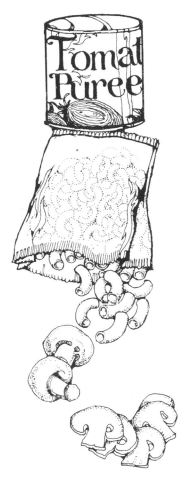

Pasta with pork stroganoff

Imperial/Metric
1¼ lb./575 g. pork fillet
2 oz./50 g. butter
4 oz./125 g. mushrooms,
 sliced
4 oz./125 g. onions, chopped
1 tablespoon flour
2½ oz./65 g. can tomato
 purée
1 teaspoon sugar
salt and pepper
¼ pint/1½ dl. soured cream
8 oz./225 g. elbow macaroni
1 tablespoon oil
bay leaf or chopped
 parsley to garnish

American
1¼ lb. pork tenderloin
¼ cup butter
1 cup sliced
 mushrooms
¾ cup chopped onion
1 tablespoon flour
5 tablespoons tomato
 paste
1 teaspoon sugar
salt and pepper
generous ½ cup soured
 cream
½ lb. elbow macaroni
1 tablespoon oil
chopped parsley to garnish

Trim the pork fillet and cut into slices about ½ inch/1 cm. thick. Fry quickly in the butter until browned, then remove from the pan. Fry the mushrooms and onions until just turning color then remove from heat and add the flour and tomato paste. Cook gently, stirring, and season with the sugar, salt and pepper. Blend in the sour cream and add the meat. If necessary, add a little stock or water so that the meat is covered. Simmer gently for 10 minutes or until the meat is tender.

Meanwhile boil the macaroni in 4 pints/2 litres of well-salted water for 14 minutes or until just cooked. Drain well and toss with the oil. Arrange the macaroni in a border round a hot serving dish, spoon the meat into the center, and garnish with chopped parsley.

Honeyed spare ribs

Imperial/Metric
3 lbs./1½ kg. pork spare
 ribs
salt
4 tablespoons clear honey
2 tablespoons soy sauce
1 tablespoon lemon juice
½ teaspoon ground ginger
8 oz./225 g. can pineapple
 chunks
4 tablespoons vinegar
1 small sweet red pepper
1 onion

American
3 lbs. pork spare ribs
salt
5 tablespoons clear honey
2 tablespoons soy sauce
1 tablespoon lemon juice
½ teaspoon ground ginger
8 oz. can pineapple
 chunks
5 tablespoons vinegar
1 small sweet red pepper
1 onion

Cut the pork into separate ribs and place in a large roasting pan. Sprinkle with salt and cook in a moderately hot oven (375°F, 190°C, Gas Mark 5) for 45 minutes, pouring off the fat as it collects. At the same time, gently melt the honey in a small saucepan together with the soy sauce, lemon juice and ginger. Lower oven heat to moderate (325°F, 170°C, Gas Mark 3), pour half the honey mixture evenly over the ribs and continue cooking for another 30 minutes, or until the ribs are well browned.

Meanwhile drain the pineapple and add pineapple syrup and vinegar to the rest of the honey mixture. Seed the red pepper and cut into chunks. Cut the onion into strips. Poach the pepper and onion in the honey mixture for 8 minutes, add the pineapple and cook for a further 2 minutes. Place spare ribs and sauce in a hot serving dish.

Tripe Italienne

Imperial/Metric
1 lb./450 g. tripe
¼ pint/1½ dl. milk
¾ pint/4 dl. water
2 teaspoons salt
1 large onion
2 tablespoons cooking oil
2 tablespoons tomato purée
¼ pint/1½ dl. dry white
 wine
½ pint/3 dl. water
1 bay leaf
pinch dried oregano
pinch grated nutmeg
¼ teaspoon garlic salt
¼ teaspoon freshly ground
 black pepper
few drops Worcestershire
 sauce
4 oz./125 g. frozen green
 peas

American
1 lb. tripe
½ cup milk
1¾ cups water
2 teaspoons salt
1 large onion
2 tablespoons cooking oil
2 tablespoons tomato paste
½ cup dry white wine
1¼ cups water
1 bay leaf
dash dried oregano
dash grated nutmeg
¼ teaspoon garlic salt
¼ teaspoon freshly ground
 black pepper
few drops Worcestershire
 sauce
¼ lb. frozen green peas

Simmer the tripe in the milk, water and salt for 1 hour. Drain and discard the cooking liquid. Cut the tripe into narrow strips. Slice the onion and fry in the oil until limp, but not browned. Add the cooked tripe, tomato paste, wine, water, bay leaf, oregano and seasonings. Simmer for 1 hour, adding more water during cooking if necessary. Stir in the green peas and simmer for a few minutes longer until the peas are cooked. Serve over steamed rice or noodles.

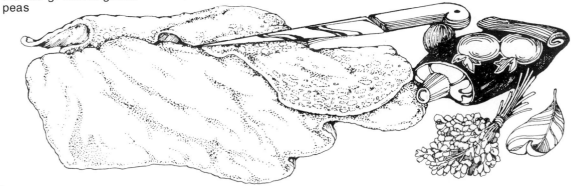

 # Chicken curry Veronique

Imperial/Metric
2 medium onions
4 chicken portions
2 oz./50 g. butter
1 tablespoon oil
2 tablespoons curry powder
¾ pint/4 dl. chicken stock
2 carrots, grated
2 tablespoons flour
5½ fl. oz./156 ml. evaporated milk
8 oz./225 g. green grapes, halved and de-seeded

American
2 medium onions
4 chicken portions
¼ cup butter
1 tablespoon oil
2 tablespoons curry powder
2 cups chicken broth
2 carrots, grated
2 tablespoons all-purpose flour
⅔ cup evaporated milk
½ lb. green grapes, halved and seeded

Finely chop the onions and fry gently with the chicken in the butter and oil until golden brown. Add the curry powder and cook for 10-15 minutes, stirring occasionally, until the chicken pieces are brown on all sides. Gradually add the stock, stirring constantly. Bring to the boil and add the carrot. Cover and simmer for 1 hour, stirring occasionally. Remove the curry from heat; whisk the flour into the evaporated milk to which enough cold water has been added to make 1¼ cups and stir quickly into the curry. Add the grapes, return to the heat and bring back to the boil. Simmer for a further 10 minutes.

40

Roast goose with apple and raisin stuffing

Imperial/Metric	American
8-10 lb./4-5 kg. goose	8-10 lb. goose
4 oz./125 g. seedless raisins	¾ cup seedless raisins
1 medium onion	1 medium onion
6 medium cooking apples	6 medium baking apples
1½ oz./40 g. butter	3 tablespoons butter
5 oz./150 g. soft white breadcrumbs	1⅔ cups soft white bread crumbs
2 oz./50 g. chopped hazelnuts, walnuts or almonds	½ cup chopped hazelnuts, walnuts or almonds
3 tablespoons chopped parsley	3 tablespoons chopped parsley
1 teaspoon dried marjoram	1 teaspoon dried marjoram
salt and pepper	salt and pepper
finely grated zest of ½ lemon	finely grated rind of ½ lemon
½ teaspoon ground mixed spices	½ teaspoon ground mixed spice
2 tablespoons clear honey	2 tablespoons clear honey
2 tablespoons water	2 tablespoons water
parsley sprigs to garnish	parsley sprigs to garnish

Wash the goose and dry thoroughly with paper towels. Pour ½ pint/3 dl. boiling water over the raisins and leave them for 20 minutes until plump and then drain. Finely chop the onion and peel, core and coarsely grate 3 of the apples. Heat the butter in a large heavy pan and cook the chopped onion over low heat until soft. Dice the goose liver and add to the onions with the raisins and grated apple. Cook for 2-3 minutes, stirring all the time until the liver is light brown. Turn into a mixing bowl and add the breadcrumbs, nuts, chopped parsley and marjoram. Mix well together and season with salt and pepper. Stuff the goose with the apple and raisin stuffing and secure with skewers. Truss the bird securely. Place the goose breast side up on a rack set in a large shallow roasting pan and roast in a moderate oven (325°F, 170°C, Gas Mark 3) for 3-3½ hours, or allow 20 minutes per lb./450 g. Pour away the fat as it collects and turn the goose halfway through cooking. Core and thickly slice the remaining apples and place in an ovenproof dish. Sprinkle with the lemon rind and mixed spices. Spoon over the honey and water. Cover the dish and place in the oven with the goose 45 minutes before the end of the cooking time. Remove the goose when ready to a heated serving dish, remove the string and skewers and garnish with the apple slices and parsley.

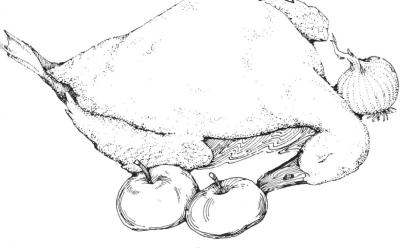

Strasbourg style goose

Imperial Metric	American
1 young goose (8 lb./4 kg.)	1 young goose (8 lb.)
2 large onions	2 large onions
3 cooking apples	3 baking apples
4 tablespoons soft brown sugar	4 tablespoons light brown sugar
3 teaspoons caraway seeds	3 teaspoons caraway seeds
salt and black pepper	salt and black pepper
2 lb./1 kg. sauerkraut	2 lb. sauerkraut
6 tablespoons beer	6 tablespoons beer

Cook the goose giblets in sufficient salted water to cover until tender. Strain off stock and reserve. Chop the onions. Peel, core and dice the apples. Cook the onion and apple for 3 minutes in the stock, add the diced liver, brown sugar, caraway seeds, pepper and sauerkraut. Season the carcass with salt and pepper, stuff with the sauerkraut mixture. Prick the goose lightly with a fork, place on a trivet in a roasting pan. Put in a moderately hot oven (400°F, 200°C, Gas Mark 6) and roast for about 2½ hours. (Allow 20 minutes per pound plus 20 minutes over.) Baste occasionally with the beer and remove excess fat from roasting pan. Serves 6-8.

Creamed turkey duchesse

Imperial/Metric
6 ozs./175 g. button
   mushrooms
1 green pepper
¼ pint/1½ dl. chicken
   stock
¾ pint/4 dl. Béchamel
   sauce
4 tablespoons double
   cream
1 egg yolk
salt and pepper
1½ teaspoons Tabasco
1½ lb./¾ kg. mashed potato
2 eggs
little milk
12 ozs./350 g. cooked
   turkey
parsley to garnish

American
1½ cups button mush-
   rooms
1 green pepper
generous ½ cup chicken
   broth
scant 2 cups white sauce
4 tablespoons whipping
   cream
1 egg yolk
salt and pepper
1½ teaspoons Tabasco
6 cups mashed potato
2 eggs
little milk
¾ lb. cooked turkey
parsley to garnish

Remove stems from the mushrooms and keep to one side. Seed the pepper and cut into chunks. Simmer the mushrooms and green pepper in a little chicken stock, until just tender, then drain and reserve liquid. Add the mushroom stems to the chicken stock and reduce rapidly, to give approximately 2 tablespoons mushroom essence. Strain this into the sauce, together with the cream and one egg yolk. Beat well and season to taste with salt, pepper and Tabasco. Heat the sauce through for 2-3 minutes, but do not allow to boil. Beat the potato until smooth and add one egg and a little milk. Fork the duchesse potato into a decorative border around the edge of an ovenproof dish, and place in a moderately hot oven (400°F, 200°C, Gas Mark 6) for 8 minutes. Beat the remaining egg and use to glaze the potato lightly. Return to the oven until golden brown. Cut the turkey into small pieces and fold into the sauce with the vegetables. Heat through together. Pile turkey mixture into the potato ring and garnish with parsley. Serves 5-6.

Turkey with chestnuts

Imperial/Metric	American
1 lb./450 g. chestnuts	1 lb. chestnuts
12 oz. pork sausage meat	¾ lb. bulk pork sausage meat
salt and pepper	salt and pepper
7-8 lb./3½ kg. turkey	8 lb. turkey
large slice fat bacon	large slice fat bacon
2 small onions, quartered	2 small onions, quartered
2 small carrots, quartered	2 small carrots, quartered
4 tablespoons brandy	4 tablespoons brandy
4 tablespoons port	4 tablespoons port
1 teaspoon cornflour	1 teaspoon cornstarch
fleurons to garnish	pastry shapes to garnish

Slit the skins of the chestnuts, place in a roasting pan in a hot oven for 10 minutes, or until the skins split. Peel and cook in boiling, salted water for 20 minutes, or until tender. Reserve a few whole chestnuts for the garnish. Chop and combine the rest of the chestnuts with the sausage-meat, season to taste and use to stuff the turkey at the neck end. Cover the turkey breast with the bacon and roast it for about 2½ hours, or until golden brown, removing the bacon for the last 30 minutes of cooking time.

Meanwhile, simmer the giblets with the onion and carrot. To serve, pour the brandy over the turkey and ignite. Strain the stock from the giblets, add the port and use to make a sauce with the juices in the roasting pan. Reduce by half and thicken with the moistened cornstarch. Reheat the chestnuts in the sauce. Serve the turkey surrounded with chestnuts and pastry shapes.

Note: If the pastry garnish is made at home, cut crescent shapes with a round biscuit cutter from puff pastry, glaze with beaten egg and place in the hottest part of the oven to bake when you remove the bacon from the turkey breast. If necessary, raise the heat slightly to brown the turkey well and encourage the pastry to rise.

★ Chicken pimiento casserole

Imperial/Metric
2 canned pimientoes
3 oz./75 g. butter
10 oz./275 g. carrots, sliced
2 onions, chopped
6 oz./175 g. mushrooms,
quartered
4 chicken portions
3 tablespoons flour
salt and pepper
1 teaspoon dried mixed
herbs
1¼ pints/7½ dl. chicken
stock
¼ pint/1½ dl. dry red wine
1 tablespoon chopped
parsley

American
2 canned pimientoes
6 tablespoons butter
2 cups sliced carrots
2 onions, chopped
generous 1 cup quartered
mushrooms
4 chicken portions
3 tablespoons all-purpose
flour
salt and pepper
1 teaspoon dried mixed
herbs
generous 3 cups chicken
broth
generous ½ cup dry red
wine
1 tablespoon chopped
parsley

Drain the pimientoes and cut into strips.
Melt the butter in a flameproof casserole
and use to fry the pimiento, carrot, onion
and mushrooms together for a few minutes. Add the chicken portions and fry
gently on both sides for about 5 minutes.
Remove the chicken. Sprinkle in the flour,
seasoning and herbs and stir thoroughly.
Gradually add the stock, stirring constantly until thick. Add the wine and
chicken, stir, bring to the boil, cover and
simmer for 30-45 minutes. Turn the
chicken once or twice during this time.
Garnish with chopped parsley.

Turkey with Claret sauce

Imperial/Metric
6-8 lb./3-4 kg. turkey
2 sticks celery
3 oz./75 g. butter
2 oz./50 g. bacon, diced
1 bottle Claret
6 oz./175 g. soft white
   breadcrumbs
2 oz./50 g. chopped
   walnuts
salt and pepper
1 egg, beaten
1 chicken stock cube
$\frac{3}{4}$ oz./20 g. flour

American
6-8 lb. turkey
2 stalks celery
6 tablespoons butter
2 slices bacon, diced
1 bottle dry red wine
2 cups fresh white bread
   crumbs
$\frac{1}{2}$ cup chopped walnuts
salt and pepper
1 egg, beaten
1 chicken bouillon cube
3 tablespoons all-purpose
   flour

Chop the celery finely and fry lightly in 2oz./50 g. of the butter with the bacon until the celery is soft but not colored. Add $\frac{1}{4}$ pint/1$\frac{1}{2}$ dl. of the wine and boil rapidly to reduce by half. Stir in the breadcrumbs, walnuts and seasoning to taste. Bind with the lightly beaten egg and sufficient stock to make a good firm stuffing consistency. Use to stuff the neck cavity of the turkey. Brush the bird lightly with oil, sprinkle with salt and pepper and cover with foil. Put the bag in a roasting pan in a moderately hot oven (375°F, 190°C, Gas Mark 5) for 2$\frac{1}{2}$-3 hours, depending on weight. Strain the clear stock from the foil into a measuring cup, add the bouillon cube and make up to $\frac{3}{4}$ pint/4 dl. with more of the wine. Make a brown roux with the remaining butter and the flour. Gradually stir in the wine stock and cook, stirring constantly, until thick and smooth. Season to taste, serve separately. Serves 8.

☆ Turkey in lemon sauce with fennel

Imperial/Metric	American
2 heads fennel, quartered	2 heads fennel, quartered
1½ oz./40 g. butter	3 tablespoons butter
1 oz./25 g. flour	¼ cup all-purpose flour
½ pint/3 dl. milk	1¼ cups milk
1 chicken stock cube	1 chicken bouillon cube
1 tablespoon lemon juice	1 tablespoon lemon juice
12 oz./350 g. cooked turkey, chopped	1½ cups chopped cooked turkey
salt and pepper	salt and pepper
1 oz./25 g. flaked almonds	¼ cup slivered almonds

Cook the fennel in boiling salted water until just tender. Melt 1 oz./25 g. of the butter, add the flour and stir over moderate heat until well blended. Gradually add the milk and the bouillon cube dissolved in 4 tablespoons boiling water. Cook, stirring constantly, for 3 minutes. Add the lemon juice, chopped turkey and the fennel. Season to taste and reheat gently. Meanwhile melt the remaining butter and fry the almonds until golden brown, sprinkling with a pinch of salt. Serve the turkey mixture topped with the fried almonds.

☆ Roast pheasant

Imperial/Metric	American
1 plump pheasant	1 plump pheasant
salt and pepper	salt and pepper
1 oz./25 g. butter	2 tablespoons butter
large rasher fat bacon	large slice bacon
¼ pint/1½ dl. red wine	½ cup red wine
little flour	little all-purpose flour
2 slices white bread	2 slices white bread
2 oz./50 g. liver pâté	2 oz. liver pâté

Season the bird inside and out with salt and pepper. Put half the butter inside the carcass, and cover the breast with the bacon. Stand on a trivet in a roasting pan. Melt the remaining butter and pour over the bird. Roast in a hot oven (450°F, 230°C, Gas Mark 8) for 10 minutes. Pour the wine over the bird, baste well, reduce heat to moderately hot (400°F, 200°C, Gas Mark 6) and return to the oven for a further 30 minutes, basting once during this time. Take the pan from the oven, remove bacon, baste with the juices, dredge lightly with flour and baste again. Raise oven heat to hot (450°F, 230°C, Gas Mark 8), return the pan and continue roasting for a further 10 minutes. Trim crusts from bread and fry or toast, then spread with the pâté. Serve the pheasant on this, surrounded by potato chips and Brussels sprouts.
Note: Ask the butcher for three tail feathers. Cut to an even length and arrange at the tail end to disguise the legs.

★ Cran-apple relish

Imperial/Metric	American
1 large cooking apple	1 large baking apple
2 tablespoons water	2 tablespoons water
1 tablespoon soft brown sugar	1 tablespoon light brown sugar
½ teaspoon ground cloves	½ teaspoon ground cloves
8 oz./225 g. cranberries	½ lb. cranberries

Peel, core and slice the apple roughly into a small saucepan. Add the water and cook over low heat until reduced to a pulp, add the sugar, cloves and cranberries and continue cooking for a further few minutes until the cranberries burst. Stir well and cool. Serve with Raised game pie.

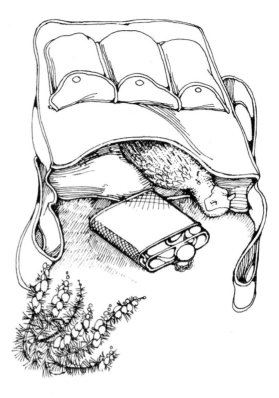

Raised game pie

Imperial/Metric
pastry:
12 oz./350 g. plain flour
½ teaspoon salt
4 oz./125 g. lard
¼ pint/1½ dl. water
1 egg yolk
filling:
1 pheasant or 2 partridges,
 boned
8 oz./225 g. lean pork,
 diced
salt and pepper
¼ teaspoon ground nutmeg
½ pint/3 dl. liquid aspic
 jelly

American
pastry:
3 cups all-purpose flour
½ teaspoon salt
½ cup lard
½ cup + 2 tablespoons
 water
1 egg yolk
filling:
1 pheasant or 2 partridges,
 boned
½ lb. lean pork, diced
salt and pepper
¼ teaspoon ground nutmeg
1 tablespoon unflavored
 gelatin dissolved in 1¼
 cups chicken broth

Sift the flour and salt into a warm bowl, and rub in 1 oz./25 g. of the fat. Place the remaining fat and water in a saucepan and heat until the fat melts. Pour into the flour with the egg yolk and beat with a wooden spoon until well blended. Knead the dough quickly on a lightly floured surface until it becomes a smooth round ball. Use the pastry while warm. Roll out two-thirds of the pastry and use to line a spring form raised pie mold. Cut the game into small pieces and layer in the pastry case with the pork, adding salt, pepper and nutmeg to each layer. Roll out remaining pastry to make a lid and seal the edges well together. Make a hole in the center and decorate with pastry trimmings. Bake in a moderately hot oven (400°F, 200°C, Gas Mark 6) for 30 minutes then lower heat to moderate (350°F, 180°C, Gas Mark 4) for a further 2-2½ hours. Cover with grease-proof paper after 1 hour's cooking. Remove mould and cool pie. Pour in the dissolved gelatin and allow to set. Serve cold with cran-apple relish.

Nutty pork crescents

Imperial/Metric
8 oz./225 g. pork sausage-
    meat
6 dates, stoned
2 oz./50 g. chopped nuts
salt and pepper
good pinch ground nutmeg
1 egg, separated
12 oz./350 g. puff pastry

American
½ lb. bulk pork sausage meat
6 dates, stoned
½ cup chopped nuts
salt and pepper
good dash ground nutmeg
1 egg, separated
¾ lb. puff paste

Mix the sausage meat with the finely chopped dates and the nuts, season well, bind with the lightly beaten egg white. Form into six sausage shapes with lightly floured hands. Roll out the pastry thinly, and cut into six squares. Place one piece of sausage meat diagonally across the corner of a pastry square, roll across and fold in the other corners. Form into a crescent shape. Beat the egg yolk with 2 tablespoons water and use to seal the parcel, turn over and brush with more egg mixture. Make up the other five parcels in the same way. Bake on a damped baking sheet in a hot oven (425°F, 220°C, Gas Mark 7) for 30 minutes. Serves 3.

Leek and bacon bake

Imperial/Metric
8 medium leeks
8 rashers streaky bacon
4 oz./125 g. Lancashire
cheese, grated

American
8 medium leeks
8 slices bacon
1 cup grated American
cheese

Trim the leeks to an even length and cut in half lengthwise. Wash well. Dice the bacon. Cook the leeks in boiling salted water, covered, until tender. Drain well. Meanwhile, fry the bacon in a heavy-based pan without added fat until golden. Use the rendered fat to grease a shallow flameproof dish. Sprinkle in a little of the grated cheese, cover with a layer of leeks, sprinkle over some of the bacon and repeat with remaining ingredients, ending with a layer of cheese. Pour over the rest of the rendered bacon fat and place under a hot grill until the cheese melts and is bubbling.

Apple and cheese canapés

Imperial/Metric
2 large dessert apples
1 large onion
2 oz./50 g. butter
1 tablespoon oil
6 slices toasting bread
grated nutmeg
6 thin slices Gouda cheese

American
2 large eating apples
1 large onion
¼ cup butter
1 tablespoon oil
6 slices toasting bread
grated nutmeg
6 thin slices Gouda cheese

Peel, core and slice the apples. Cut the onion into thin slices and separate into rings. Fry the apple slices gently in half the butter until light golden. Remove and keep warm. Add the oil to the pan and use to fry the onion rings gently until golden. Lightly toast the bread and butter on one side. Place a little onion on each slice, reserving good rings for the garnish. Divide the cooked apple slices among the six slices of toast, sprinkle with grated nutmeg, cover with a slice of cheese and top with a few onion rings. Place under a hot grill until the cheese begins to melt and the onion rings are brown. Serves 3.

Ham and turkey mousse

Imperial/Metric
1 tablespoon gelatine
2 tablespoons cold water
1 chicken stock cube
½ pint/3 dl. boiling water
1 teaspoon lemon juice
pinch salt
pinch dry mustard
4 oz./125 g. cooked turkey
4 oz./125 g. cooked ham
1 tablespoon grated onion
¼ pint/1½ dl. double cream
2 egg whites

American
1 tablespoon unflavored gelatin
2 tablespoons cold water
1 chicken bouillon cube
1¼ cups boiling water
1 teaspoon lemon juice
dash salt
dash dry mustard
¼ lb. cooked turkey
¼ lb. cooked ham
1 tablespoon minced onion
⅔ cup whipping cream
2 egg whites

Soften the gelatin in the cold water. Dissolve the bouillon cube in the boiling water and add to the gelatin. Stir until dissolved. Add the lemon juice, salt and dry mustard. Chill until slightly thickened. Meanwhile mince the turkey and ham very finely. Beat the partially set gelatin until smooth. Stir in the minced turkey, ham and onion. Whip the cream lightly. Beat the egg whites until very stiff. Fold the whipped cream and egg whites into the meat and gelatin mixture. Spoon into a 2 pint/generous 1 litre jelly mold. Chill until set. Unmold, cut in wedges and serve with cranberry sauce.

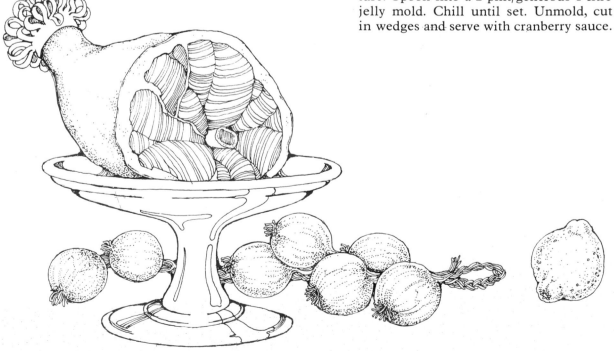

Spinach noodle cake

Imperial/Metric
2 lb./1 kg. spinach
8 oz./225 g. noodles
1 oz./25 g. butter
6 oz./175 g. cheese, grated
3 eggs
¾ pint/4 dl. milk
½ teaspoon ground mace
salt and black pepper

American
2 lb. spinach
½ lb. noodles
2 tablespoons butter
1½ cups grated cheese
3 eggs
scant 2 cups milk
½ teaspoon ground mace
salt and black pepper

Wash and cook the spinach in just sufficient boiling salted water to prevent it from burning, drain and chop finely. Cook the noodles in plenty of boiling salted water for 8 minutes, or until just tender but not soft. Drain well, and toss in half the butter. Grease an ovenproof dish with remaining butter put a layer of spinach in the bottom, sprinkle in half the cheese, then add the noodles, a little more cheese, the remaining spinach and the rest of the cheese. Beat the eggs with the milk, add seasoning and pour over the dish. Bake in a moderate oven (350°F, 180°C, Gas Mark 4) for 30-40 minutes.

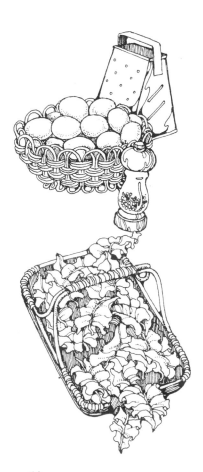

Sausage and butter bean quickies

Imperial/Metric
1 lb./450 g. sausages
16 oz./450 g. can butter
  beans
$\frac{1}{4}$ pint/1$\frac{1}{2}$ dl. milk approx.
2 oz./50 g. butter
1 large onion, sliced
1 tablespoon flour
salt and pepper
2 oz./50 g. cheese, grated
chopped parsley

American
1 lb. sausages
1 lb. can butter beans
$\frac{1}{2}$ cup milk approx.
$\frac{1}{4}$ cup butter
1 large onion, sliced
1 tablespoon flour
salt and pepper
$\frac{1}{2}$ cup cheese, grated
chopped parsley

Grill or fry the sausages until nicely brown all over. Strain the liquid from the beans and make up to $\frac{1}{2}$ pint/3 dl. with milk. Heat the butter in a saucepan and fry the onion gently until just colored, remove from the heat and stir in the flour. Gradually blend in the liquid and bring to the boil, stirring constantly. Cook gently for 3 minutes. Mix in the butter beans, season to taste, and pour into a shallow ovenproof dish. Arrange the sausages on top and scatter the grated cheese over. Cook under the grill until golden and bubbling. Garnish with chopped parsley.

Vegetables and salads

When delicate salad vegetables are scarce and expensive, combine them with thinly sliced cabbage, white or red; tiny raw florets of cauliflower; or crisp shredded Brussels sprouts. Nuts and the citrus fruits in full season too add interest to winter salads. Root vegetables deserve more attention, and can easily be prepared to make a separate course, worthy to serve on its own. Try this selection for a start.

Polish beet salad

Imperial/Metric
4 oz./125 g. slice cooked tongue
1 large beetroot
4 fillets salt herring
4 tablespoons French dressing
1 hard-boiled egg
1 tablespoon chopped parsley

American
$\frac{1}{4}$ lb. slice cooked tongue
1 large beet
4 fillets salt herring
4 tablespoons Italian dressing
1 hard cooked egg
1 tablespoon chopped parsley

Roughly chop the tongue, dice the beet and quarter the herring fillets. Toss the beet, herring and tongue in the salad dressing. Reserve four center slices of the egg for garnish, chop the rest roughly and put in the bottom of a salad bowl. Cover with half the tossed ingredients and sprinkle with a little parsley. Fill up the bowl with the remaining ingredients, garnish with the reserved egg slices and the rest of the parsley.

Red coleslaw with celery

Imperial/Metric
1 small red cabbage
3 large oranges
½ head celery
2 oz./50 g. walnut halves
salt and pepper
½ teaspoon mild continental
  mustard
1 tablespoon oil

American
1 small red cabbage
3 large oranges
½ head celery
½ cup walnut halves
salt and pepper
½ teaspoon mild mustard
1 tablespoon oil

Shred the cabbage finely, removing the core and thick stems. Peel 2 of the oranges and divide into segments, discarding the pith and membrane. Chop the celery into short lengths and mix with the orange segments, cabbage and walnuts. Squeeze the juice from the remaining orange, season to taste with salt, pepper and mustard and beat in the oil. Pour over the salad ingredients and toss well.

Honeyed carrots

Imperial/Metric
4 large carrots
2 oz./50 g. butter
1 tablespoon made
  mustard
2 oz./50 ml. honey
1 tablespoon chopped
  almonds

American
4 large carrots
¼ cup butter or margarine
1 tablespoon prepared
  mustard
¼ cup honey
1 tablespoon chopped
  almonds

Peel and cut the carrots diagonally into 1 inch/25 mm. slices. Cook in boiling salted water for 15 minutes. While the carrots are cooking, combine the butter, mustard and honey. Cook over low heat for 3 minutes until thoroughly blended. Drain the carrots. Pour the sauce over and sprinkle with the chopped almonds.

Chicory and orange salad

Imperial/Metric
2 large oranges
4 heads chicory
5 oz./150 ml. carton
   natural yogurt
salt and pepper

American
2 large oranges
4 heads Belgian endive
$\frac{2}{3}$ cup unflavored yogurt
salt and pepper

Grate the rind of one orange, peel and divide both oranges into segments. Trim and divide the chicory heads into separate leaves. Reserve 10 or 12 leaves for the garnish and chop the rest roughly. Place the orange segments and chopped chicory in a bowl, toss with the yogurt, and part of the grated rind, reserving a little for the garnish. Season to taste. Turn the mixture into a serving dish and push chicory leaves down the sides at regular intervals. Sprinkle the remaining orange rind on the top.

Savory vegetable medley

Imperial/Metric	American
4 oz./125 g. carrots	4 oz. carrots
4 oz./125 g. turnip	4 oz. turnip
4 oz./125 g. celeriac	4 oz. celeriac
8 oz./225 g. white cabbage	½ lb. cabbage
1 leek	1 leek
2 oz./50 g. butter	¼ cup butter or margarine
4 oz./125 g. lean bacon	4 oz. bacon
1 chicken stock cube	1 chicken bouillon cube
½ pint/3 dl. boiling water	1¼ cups boiling water
salt and pepper	salt and pepper
1 bay leaf	1 bay leaf
2 oz./50 g. frozen green peas	½ cup frozen green peas
1 oz./25 g. cheese, grated	¼ cup grated cheese

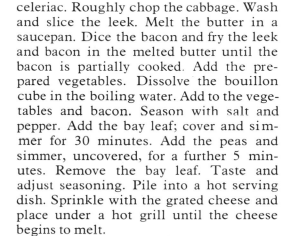

Peel and dice the carrots, turnip and celeriac. Roughly chop the cabbage. Wash and slice the leek. Melt the butter in a saucepan. Dice the bacon and fry the leek and bacon in the melted butter until the bacon is partially cooked. Add the prepared vegetables. Dissolve the bouillon cube in the boiling water. Add to the vegetables and bacon. Season with salt and pepper. Add the bay leaf; cover and simmer for 30 minutes. Add the peas and simmer, uncovered, for a further 5 minutes. Remove the bay leaf. Taste and adjust seasoning. Pile into a hot serving dish. Sprinkle with the grated cheese and place under a hot grill until the cheese begins to melt.

Finnish turnip loaf

Imperial/Metric	American
1 lb./450 g. turnips	1 lb. turnips
2 eggs	2 eggs
1 teaspoon sugar	1 teaspoon sugar
pinch pepper	pinch pepper
pinch grated nutmeg	pinch grated nutmeg
2 fl. oz./50 ml. single cream	¼ cup coffee cream
4 tablespoons soft bread-crumbs	4 tablespoons soft bread crumbs
1 tablespoon melted butter	1 tablespoon melted butter

Peel, dice and cook the turnips in boiling salted water until tender. Drain and mash. Beat the eggs lightly and add to the mashed turnips along with the sugar, pepper, nutmeg and cream. Spoon into a buttered 1 lb./450 g. loaf pan. Combine the breadcrumbs and melted butter. Sprinkle over the turnip mixture. Bake in a moderately hot oven (375°F, 190°C, Gas Mark 5) for 45 minutes.

Sovereign salad

Imperial/Metric	American
1 lb./450 g. red cabbage	1 lb. red cabbage
1 green-skinned dessert apple	1 green-skinned eating apple
1 celery heart	1 celery heart
4 sprigs watercress	4 sprigs watercress
dressing:	dressing:
½ teaspoon salt and ¼ teaspoon pepper	½ teaspoon salt and ¼ teaspoon pepper
½ teaspoon dry mustard	½ teaspoon dry mustard
pinch castor sugar	dash granulated sugar
1 tablespoon lemon juice	1 tablespoon lemon juice
2 tablespoons oil	2 tablespoons oil

Shred the cabbage finely into a bowl, discarding the core and thick stems. Core and slice the apple thinly. Slice the celery heart finely, and chop up the watercress, reserving 4 tiny top sprigs for the garnish. To make the dressing, stir the seasonings and sugar into the lemon juice and gradually beat in the oil. Toss the apple, celery and chopped watercress in the dressing until well coated. Divide the shredded cabbage between four individual salad bowls, cover with the celery mixture and dressing and top with the reserved sprigs of watercress.

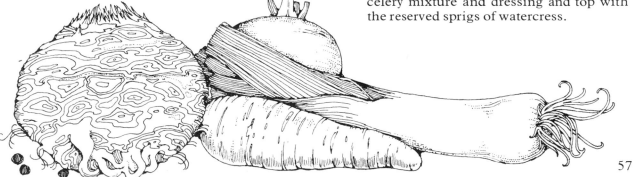

Desserts

Hot puddings are top of our list, but space must be found as well for the rich desserts and cakes proper to the season. Dieters are not forgotten (there's even a Dieters' Christmas pudding) but might be forgiven for a temporary lapse when mincemeat, rich plum cake and other such delights appear on the festive menu.

Chinese toffee apples

Imperial/Metric
1 tablespoon sesame seeds
4 dessert apples
1 tablespoon cornflour
4 oz./125 g. sugar
2 tablespoons corn oil

American
1 tablespoon sesame seeds
4 eating apples
1 tablespoon cornstarch
½ cup granulated sugar
2 tablespoons corn oil

Spread the sesame seeds on a sheet of foil and toast under a hot grill until golden. Peel, core and cut the apples into small chunks and toss them in cornstarch. Dissolve the sugar slowly in the oil until it becomes a thick syrup with a little oil floating on top and pale golden brown in color. Stir in the sesame seeds. Drop in a few apple chunks at a time, remove with a fork and pile up in a warm serving dish. To serve, turn a spoonful of toffee-coated chunks at a time into a bowl of iced water and immediately remove with a slotted spoon.

Beignets

Imperial/Metric
1 packet boudoir biscuits,
  crushed
4 oz./125 g. cream cheese
2 tablespoons single cream
3 tablespoons flour
2 eggs
1 tablespoon brandy or rum
oil for frying
castor sugar for dredging

American
1 package ladyfingers,
  crushed
4 oz. cream cheese
2 tablespoons coffee cream
3 tablespoons all-purpose
  flour
2 eggs
1 tablespoon brandy or rum
oil for frying
granulated sugar for
  dredging

Beat all the ingredients together and let stand for 15 minutes. Heat the oil until a piece of the paste begins to frizzle as soon as it is immersed in the oil. Form the mixture into pieces about the size of a walnut. Add a few at a time to the oil in a frying basket, cooking in batches. When golden brown remove carefully on to paper towels to drain. Keep warm until all the beignets are cooked. Serve dredged with sugar or with apricot jam.

Apple mountains

Imperial/Metric
8 large dessert apples
5 oz./150 g. butter
5 oz./150 g. castor sugar
3 eggs
pinch salt
1 teaspoon vanilla extract
1¼ cups flour
8 Maraschino cherries

American
8 large eating apples
⅔ cup butter
⅔ cup granulated sugar
3 eggs
pinch salt
1 teaspoon vanilla extract
1¼ cups all-purpose flour
8 Maraschino cherries

Peel and core the apples. Melt 1 oz./25 g. of the butter in a flameproof dish large enough to take all eight apples. Turn apples in the butter over moderate heat until golden on all sides. Sprinkle with 1 oz./25 g. of the sugar, cover and continue cooking over low heat for 7-10 minutes until just tender. Meanwhile beat together the remaining butter and sugar and gradually add the eggs, salt and vanilla extract. Blend in the flour. Use the mixture to cover the apples and bake in a moderate oven (350°F, 180°C, Gas Mark 4) for 40-45 minutes, until the surface is golden brown and resilient to the touch. If necessary cover the edges with foil and leave the center exposed for another 10 minutes cooking as the edges tend to over-brown before center is fully cooked. Decorate with the cherries and serve hot. Serves 8.

Mincemeat cobbler

Imperial/Metric
8 small slices white bread
3 oz./75 g. shredded suet
3 oz./75 g. demerara or
    soft brown sugar
1 teaspoon ground
    cinnamon
1 lb./450 g. cooking pears
grated zest and juice of
    1 lemon
8 oz./225 g. mincemeat

American
8 small slices white bread
½ cup finely chopped suet
6 tablespoons light
    brown sugar
1 teaspoon ground
    cinnamon
1 lb. winter pears
grated rind and juice of
    1 lemon
1 cup mincemeat

Using a 2½ inch/6 cm. cutter, cut out 7 rounds from 7 slices of the bread. Make breadcrumbs from leftover slice and pieces of bread. Mix together suet, sugar and cinnamon. Combine the breadcrumbs with two-thirds of the suet mixture. Sprinkle one half over the base of a greased 1½-2 pint/1 litre round ovenproof dish. Bake in a moderately hot oven (400°F, 200°C, Gas Mark 6) for 10 minutes. Peel, core and grate pears. Combine with the lemon rind and juice, and the mincemeat. Spread half the fruit mixture over the crumb base and cover with remaining breadcrumbs, then the remaining fruit mixture. Arrange rounds of bread overlapping slightly on top leaving a round of fruit mixture showing in the center. Sprinkle remaining third of suet, sugar and cinnamon mixture over the bread and bake for 20-25 minutes until top is crisp and golden. Serves 4-6.

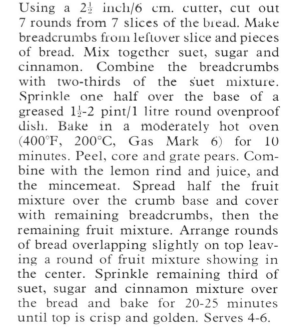

Golden grapefruit sponge

Imperial/Metric
5 oz./150 g. self-raising
  flour
pinch of salt
3 oz./75 g. butter
4 oz./125 g. castor sugar
2 eggs, beaten
1 tablespoon milk
grated zest of $\frac{1}{2}$ grapefruit

American
1$\frac{1}{4}$ cups all-purpose flour
1$\frac{1}{4}$ teaspoons baking
  powder
pinch salt
6 tablespoons butter
$\frac{1}{2}$ cup granulated sugar
2 eggs, beaten
1 tablespoon milk
grated rind of $\frac{1}{2}$ grapefruit

Sieve the flour and salt together. In a separate bowl cream the butter and sugar until light and fluffy. Gradually add the eggs, alternately with the flour. Beat in the milk and grapefruit rind. Pour the mixture into a greased pudding basin and cover with foil. Steam for 1$\frac{1}{2}$ hours, turn out and serve with Grapefruit sauce.

Grapefruit sauce

Imperial/Metric
2 grapefruit
2-4 tablespoons golden
  syrup
1 teaspoon arrowroot
knob of butter

American
2 grapefruit
2-4 tablespoons corn
  syrup
1 teaspoon arrowroot
knob of butter

Thinly pare the rind of one grapefruit and squeeze the juice from both. Place in a saucepan with corn syrup to taste and bring to the boil. Moisten the arrowroot with 2 tablespoons cold water, add to the pan and bring to the boil, stirring constantly until sauce clears. Beat in the butter and serve with Golden grapefruit sponge.

Cider and fruit bread pudding

Imperial/Metric
$\frac{3}{4}$ pint/4 dl. cider
1 oz./25 g. sultanas
1 oz./25 g. currants
2 oz./50 g. seedless raisins
1 oz./25 g. butter
1 oz./25 g. soft brown
  sugar
3 oz./75 g. fresh white
  breadcrumbs
2 eggs, separated
2-3 oz./50-75 g. castor
  sugar

American
scant 2 cups apple cider
$\frac{1}{4}$ cup golden raisins
scant $\frac{1}{4}$ cup currants
scant $\frac{1}{2}$ cup dark seedless
  raisins
2 tablespoons butter
2 tablespoons light brown
  sugar
1$\frac{1}{2}$ cups fresh white bread
  crumbs
2 eggs, separated
4-6 tablespoons granulated
  sugar

Pour $\frac{1}{2}$ pint/3 dl./1$\frac{1}{4}$ cups cider over the dried fruit, allow to stand overnight then drain and reserve the liquid. Add extra cider to bring the liquid up to $\frac{1}{2}$ pint/3dl./ 1$\frac{1}{4}$ cups again and heat with the fat and brown sugar until the sugar dissolves. Stir in the breadcrumbs and heat for a further 2 minutes. Remove from the heat and stir in the egg yolks, one at a time. Spoon half the bread mixture into a greased 1$\frac{1}{2}$ pint/1 litre/1 quart ovenproof dish, cover with half the fruit and the remaining bread mixture. Bake in the center of a moderately hot oven (375°F, 190°C, Gas Mark 5) for 15 minutes, or until set. Beat the egg whites until very stiff and fold in the sugar. Place remaining fruit on top of the pudding and pile the meringue on top. Return to the oven for about 10 minutes, until the meringue is lightly browned. Serves 4-6.

☆ Chestnut soufflé

Imperial/Metric
1 lb./450 g. chestnuts
4 oz./125 g. castor sugar
little milk
4 eggs, separated
1 tablespoon flour
few drops vanilla essence

American
1 lb. chestnuts
½ cup granulated sugar
little milk
4 eggs, separated
1 tablespoon all-purpose
   flour
few drops vanilla extract

Butter an ovenproof soufflé dish. Cook the chestnuts (see page 43) and reduce to a smooth purée with the sugar and just sufficient milk to make the mixture a smooth paste. Beat in the egg yolks, one at a time, sprinkling in a little flour with each addition. Beat the egg whites until stiff and fold lightly into the chestnut mixture with the vanilla extract. Pour into the prepared dish and bake in a moderately hot oven (375°F, 190°C, Gas Mark 5) for about 35 minutes, until well risen and golden brown. Serve at once with Coffee liqueur sauce.

☆ Coffee liqueur sauce

Imperial/Metric
½ pint/3 dl. strong black
   coffee
pinch salt
2 oz./50 g. sugar
4 tablespoons coffee
   liqueur
2 teaspoons arrowroot
1 egg yolk
knob of butter

American
1¼ cups strong black
   coffee
dash salt
¼ cup granulated sugar
4 tablespoons coffee
   liqueur
2 teaspoons arrowroot
1 egg yolk
1 tablespoon butter

Heat the coffee, salt and sugar to boiling point and add the liqueur. Moisten the arrowroot with a little cold water, add to the pan and stir, over moderate heat, until the mixture clears. Remove sauce from heat, stir in the egg yolk quickly and then the butter to give the sauce a gloss.

Light Christmas pudding

Imperial/Metric
4 oz./125 g. soft brown
  sugar
7 oz./200 g. plain flour
1 teaspoon bicarbonate of
  soda
½ teaspoon salt
½ teaspoon ground
  cinnamon
½ teaspoon grated nutmeg
½ teaspoon ground mixed
  spices
4 oz./125 g. seedless raisins
4 oz./125 g. currants
4 oz./125 g. sultanas
4 oz./125 g. chopped mixed
  peel
2½ fl. oz./65 ml. corn oil
3 fl. oz./75 ml. milk
4 tablespoons brandy
2 eggs

American
½ cup light brown sugar
1¾ cups all-purpose flour
1 teaspoon baking soda
½ teaspoon salt
½ teaspoon ground
  cinnamon
½ teaspoon grated nutmeg
½ teaspoon ground mixed
  spice
¾ cup dark seedless raisins
⅔ cup currants
¾ cup golden raisins
generous 1 cup chopped
  mixed peel
⅓ cup corn oil
⅓ cup milk
4 tablespoons brandy
2 eggs

Grease a 2 pint/1 litre/1 quart pudding basin and coat with brown sugar. Sieve the dry ingredients into a bowl and stir in the fruit. Whisk together the corn oil, milk, brandy and eggs and stir into the dry ingredients. Mix well. Turn into the prepared basin. Cover with waxed paper and foil and steam for 6 hours. Allow to cool. Remove the paper and re-cover with a clean dry cloth. When required steam for a further 1½ hours and serve with Marsala sauce, or Hot rum sauce.

Marsala sauce

Imperial/Metric
½ oz./15 g. cornflour
½ pint/3 dl. milk
2 tablespoons sugar
4 tablespoons Marsala
½ teaspoon almond essence
knob of butter

American
1 tablespoon cornstarch
1¼ cups milk
2 tablespoons granulated
  sugar
4 tablespoons Marsala
½ teaspoon almond extract
1 tablespoon butter

Moisten the cornstarch with 2 tablespoons of the milk. Heat the remaining milk gradually to boiling point with the sugar. Pour on to the blended cornstarch, stir well and return to the pan. Bring to the boil again, stirring constantly. Add the Marsala and almond extract and simmer, stirring constantly, for a further 3 minutes. Beat in the butter and remove from the heat. Makes ½ pint/3 dl./1¼ cups sauce.

Hot rum sauce

Imperial/Metric
8 oz./225 g. soft brown
  sugar
3 fl. oz./75 ml. honey
pinch salt
4 oz./125 g. butter
2 fl. oz./50 ml. hot water
3 fl. oz./75 ml. rum

American
1 cup brown sugar
⅓ cup honey
dash salt
½ cup butter
¼ cup hot water
⅓ cup rum

In a small saucepan, heat the brown sugar, honey, salt, butter and water together until it begins to boil. Remove from the heat and stir in the rum. Makes ½ pint/3 dl./1¼ cups sauce.

Dieters' Christmas pudding

Imperial/Metric
1 packet Rise & Shine
  lemon drink
2 tablespoons water
$\frac{1}{4}$ pint/1$\frac{1}{2}$ dl. whipping cream
8 oz./225 g. cottage cheese
finely grated zest of 1
  orange
1 oz/25 g. sultanas
1 oz./25 g. currants
1 oz./25 g. glacé cherries,
  quartered
$\frac{1}{2}$ oz./15 g. gelatine
glacé cherries and angelica
  to decorate

American
1 packet Rise & Shine
  lemon drink
2 tablespoons water
$\frac{1}{2}$ cup whipping cream
1 cup cottage cheese
finely grated rind of 1
  orange
$\frac{1}{4}$ cup golden raisins
$\frac{1}{4}$ cup currants
$\frac{1}{4}$ cup quartered candied
  cherries
1 tablespoon unflavored
  gelatin
candied cherries and
  angelica to decorate

Mix the drink powder and water together. Whip the cream and force the cottage cheese through a sieve. Combine the cheese, orange rind, lemon drink and fruit and fold in the cream. Dissolve the gelatin in 3 tablespoons water in a bowl over a pan of hot water. Cool, then add to the cheese mixture and mix well. Pour into a rinsed 1 pint/$\frac{1}{2}$ litre bowl/small mold and chill until set. To serve, dip the mold into warm water for a few seconds, then turn pudding out on a serving plate. Decorate with glacé cherries and angelica. Serves 6-8.

Note: For long term storage wrap in foil before freezing. Remove, unwrap and place on a serving dish when required.

Beat 'n bake Christmas cake

Imperial/Metric
1 lb./450 g. mixed dried fruit
4 oz./125 g. candied and glacé fruit, chopped
7 oz./200 g. flour
1 teaspoon ground mixed spices (nutmeg, cinnamon, etc)
2 oz./50 g. chopped almonds
2 oz./50 g. ground almonds
4 oz./125 g. soft margarine
4 oz./125 g. soft brown sugar
2 tablespoons treacle
3 large eggs
1 miniature bottle Apricot brandy

American
3 cups mixed dried fruit
generous 1 cup mixed candied fruits, chopped
1¾ cups all-purpose flour
1 teaspoon ground mixed spices (nutmeg, cinnamon, etc)
½ cup chopped almonds
generous ¼ cup ground almonds
½ cup soft margarine
½ cup light brown sugar
2 tablespoons molasses
3 large eggs
1 miniature bottle Apricot brandy

Quite simply, place all the ingredients together in a large mixing bowl and beat with a wooden spoon until too tired to continue (3 minutes is the minimum). Grease and line an 8 inch/20 cm. cake pan and protect by wrapping a double layer of brown paper around the outside, to come 2 inches/5 cm. above the top of the tin. Fill the pan, smooth the top of the mixture and set the pan in the oven on a pad of newspaper. Bake in a cool oven (275°F, 150°C, Gas Mark 1) for about 3 hours, until no sound of humming is heard from the cake. Cool, and store in an airtight tin.

Fruited savarin

Imperial/Metric
½ oz./15 g. fresh yeast, or 2 teaspoons dried yeast
¼ pint/1½ dl. warm milk
5 oz./150 g. plain flour
¼ teaspoon salt
½ oz./15 g. castor sugar
1 egg, beaten
1 oz./25 g. butter
2 oz./50 g. glacé cherries
2 oz./50 g. sultanas
2 oz./50 g. seedless raisins
little butter for greasing tin
½ oz./15 g. flaked almonds
syrup:
8 oz./225 g. granulated sugar
½ pint/3 dl. water
2 tablespoons sweet sherry
¼ pint/1½ dl. double cream

American
1 tablespoon fresh yeast or 2 teaspoons dried yeast
generous ½ cup warm milk
1¼ cups all-purpose flour
¼ teaspoon salt
1 tablespoon granulated sugar
1 egg, beaten
2 tablespoons butter
¼ cup quartered candied cherries
scant ½ cup golden raisins
scant ½ cup seedless raisins
little butter for greasing tin
2 tablespoons slivered almonds
syrup:
1 cup sugar
1¼ cups water
2 tablespoons sweet sherry
½ cup whipping cream

Combine the yeast, milk and 1 oz./25g. flour in a large bowl, beat until smooth then let stand until frothy, about 20 minutes for fresh yeast, 30 minutes for dried yeast. Add remaining flour, salt, sugar, egg and softened butter to the yeast mixture and, using a wooden spoon, beat thoroughly for 3-4 minutes. Stir in the cherries, golden and dark raisins. Grease a 7 inch/18 cm. ring mold with a little butter and sprinkle with the almonds. Spoon mixture into the mold and cover with foil or plastic. Allow to rise in a warm place for about 45 minutes to 1 hour, until mixture almost reaches the top of the mold. Bake in a moderately hot oven (400°F, 200°C, Gas Mark 6) for about 25 minutes, until firm to the touch and golden brown. Remove from the oven and leave in the mold for 5 minutes, turn out on a wire rack to cool. To make the syrup, dissolve the granulated sugar in the water, boil for 2 minutes. Remove from the heat and stir in the sherry. Return savarin to the mold, spoon half the syrup over it. Spoon over more syrup every 30 minutes until it has all been absorbed. Invert the mold on a serving dish and let stand for several hours, or overnight, until required. To serve, whip the cream until thick, remove mold from savarin and spoon the cream into the center. Serves 6.

Plum cake with rum syrup

Imperial/Metric
4 oz./125 g. plain flour
½ teaspoon baking powder
½ teaspoon salt
3 oz./75 g. margarine
4 oz./125 g. castor sugar
3 eggs
½ teaspoon vanilla essence
3 oz./75 g. stoned prunes, chopped
3 oz./75 g. glacé cherries
3 oz./75 g. chopped candied peel
3 oz./75 g. sultanas
2 oz./50 g. flaked almonds
syrup:
8 oz./225 g. sugar
½ pint/3 dl. water
2 tablespoons rum
glacé cherries and angelica to decorate

American
1 cup all-purpose flour
½ teaspoon baking powder
½ teaspoon salt
6 tablespoons margarine
½ cup granulated sugar
3 eggs
½ teaspoon vanilla extract
generous ½ cup chopped pitted prunes
¾ cup chopped candied cherries
½ cup chopped candied peel
generous ½ cup golden raisins
¼ cup slivered almonds
syrup:
1 cup granulated sugar
1¼ cups water
2 tablespoons rum
candied cherries and angelica to
    decorate

Sift the flour, baking powder and salt.
Cream together the margarine and sugar
until light and fluffy. Add one egg at a
time, beating each in thoroughly. If mixture shows signs of curdling, beat in a
little of the sifted flour. Beat in the vanilla
extract. Fold in the flour, fruit and nuts.
Turn the mixture into a well greased ring
mold and bake in a cool oven (300°F,
150°C, Gas Mark 2) for 2½ hours. Remove
from the oven and cool for 5 minutes
before turning out. To make the syrup,
dissolve the sugar in the water over gentle
heat. Bring to the boil and continue boiling for 2 minutes. Remove from the heat
and stir in the rum. Return the cake to the
mold and prick the surface. Spoon half
the hot syrup over it and allow to stand for
30 minutes. Spoon more syrup over at intervals of one hour until it is all absorbed.
Invert the cake on to a serving dish and
decorate with cherries and angelica leaves.

 # Raisin lattice pie

Imperial/Metric
8 oz./225 g. plain flour
½ teaspoon salt
4 oz./125 g. whipped white
 cooking fat
2 tablespoons water
1 egg white
filling:
2 medium oranges
1 oz./25 g. cornflour
8 oz./225 g. seedless raisins
2 oz./50 g. brown sugar
2 oz./50 g. butter

American
2 cups all-purpose flour
½ teaspoon salt
½ cup vegetable shortening
2 tablespoons water
1 egg white
filling:
2 medium oranges
2 tablespoons cornstarch
1½ cups dark seedless
 raisins
¼ cup brown sugar
¼ cup butter

Sift the flour and salt into a bowl. Add the fat and water and mix with a fork until a ball of dough is formed. Knead lightly. Line a 9 inch/22 cm. pie pan with three quarters of the pastry and roll the remainder into six ½ inch/1 cm. strips. Dampen pastry edges with egg white. Grate the orange rind and squeeze the juice. Add water to juice to make 1¼ cups. Blend the cornstarch with 2 tablespoons of the liquid. Boil the remainder with the raisins and sugar. Add the moistened cornstarch and bring to the boil, stirring constantly. Add the butter and orange rind, cool and pour into the prepared pastry case. Place the pastry strips in a lattice pattern over the filling. Brush with egg white and bake in a moderately hot oven (400°F, 200°C, Gas Mark 6) for 30 minutes. Serve hot or cold.

Spicy carrot cake with cream cheese frosting

Imperial/Metric
4 oz./125 g. flour
8 oz./225 g. sugar
1 teaspoon bicarbonate of
  soda
¼ teaspoon salt
1 teaspoon ground
  cinnamon
½ teaspoon ground
  allspice
4 fl. oz./125 ml. cooking
  oil
2 eggs
½ lb./225 g. finely grated
  raw carrots
frosting:
3 oz./85 g. cream cheese
2 oz./50 g. butter
8 oz./225 g. icing sugar,
  sieved
1 teaspoon vanilla essence
¼ teaspoon grated nutmeg

American
1 cup all-purpose flour
1 cup granulated sugar
1 teaspoon baking soda
¼ teaspoon salt
1 teaspoon ground
  cinnamon
½ teaspoon ground
  allspice
½ cup cooking oil
2 eggs
1¼ cups finely grated raw
  carrots
frosting:
3 oz. package cream
  cheese
¼ cup butter
2 cups sifted confectioners'
  sugar
1 teaspoon vanilla extract
¼ teaspoon grated nutmeg

Grease and lightly flour one 7 inch/18 cm. deep cake pan. Sift the flour, sugar, baking soda, salt and spices into a mixing bowl. Stir in the oil (the mixture will be very thick). Add the eggs, one at a time, beating well after each addition. Stir in the grated carrots and spread the batter evenly in the prepared cake pan. Bake in a moderate oven (350°F, 180°C, Gas Mark 4) for 45 minutes. Cool in the pan for 10 minutes then turn out on a wire rack. To make the frosting, soften the cream cheese with the butter. Beat the confectioners' sugar, vanilla extract and nutmeg into the creamed mixture. Spread frosting on the top and sides of the cake and mark into swirls. If a thinner consistency is desired, add a little milk.

Orange gingerbread fingers

Imperial/Metric
4 fl. oz./110 ml. treacle
2 eggs, beaten
2 oz./50 g. candied orange
  peel, chopped
2 oz./50 g. stem ginger,
  chopped
grated zest and juice of 1
  orange
4 oz./125 g. castor sugar
12 oz./350 g. plain flour
pinch salt
1 teaspoon bicarbonate of
  soda
1 teaspoon ground cinnamon
2 teaspoons ground ginger
4 oz./125 g. butter
little ginger syrup

American
½ cup molasses
2 eggs, beaten
⅓ cup chopped candied rind
⅓ cup chopped preserved
  ginger
grated rind and juice of 1
  orange
½ cup granulated sugar
3 cups all-purpose flour
dash salt
1 teaspoon baking soda
1 teaspoon ground cinnamon
2 teaspoons ground ginger
½ cup butter
little ginger syrup

Warm the molasses and stir in the eggs, chopped peel, chopped ginger, orange rind and juice and the sugar. Sift the flour, salt, baking soda and the spices into a bowl and rub in the butter. Stir in the molasses mixture and mix well. Add a little ginger syrup if necessary to give a pouring consistency. Transfer the mixture to a lined 9 inch/22 cm. square cake tin and bake in a moderate oven (325°F, 170°C, Gas Mark 3) for 1-1¼ hours. Serve cut into fingers.

☆ Hazelnut cream gâteau

Imperial/Metric
4 oz./125 g. butter
4 oz./125 g. castor sugar
2 eggs
4 oz./125 g. self-raising
  flour
pinch salt
2 oz./50 g. chopped
  hazelnuts
few hazelnut kernels
½ pint/3 dl. double cream
8 oz./225 g. greengage jam

American
½ cup butter
½ cup granulated sugar
2 eggs
1 cup all-purpose flour
1 teaspoon baking powder
dash salt
½ cup chopped hazelnuts
few hazelnut kernels
1¼ cups whipping cream
1 cup greengage plum jam

Cream the butter and sugar until light and fluffy. Gradually beat in the eggs, adding a teaspoon of flour with the last addition. Sift the flour and salt and fold into the creamed mixture. Divide between two greased 7 inch/18 cm. cake pans and bake in a moderate oven (350°F, 180°C, Gas Mark 4) for 25-30 minutes. Cool on a wire rack. Place the chopped and whole hazelnuts on a sheet of foil and toast under a hot grill until brown. Whip the cream until thick. Spread jam on one sponge layer and cover with a little of the cream. Place the other sponge layer on top and carefully spread a thin layer of cream over the sides of the cake. Press chopped hazelnuts against the sides to coat. Cover the top of the cake with greengage jam. Place remaining cream in a pastry bag fitted with a star nozzle and make even lines of cream across the cake. Make rosettes around the edge of the cake and top each rosette with a whole hazelnut.
Note: The recipe can be varied by using other kinds of jam such as seedless raspberry.

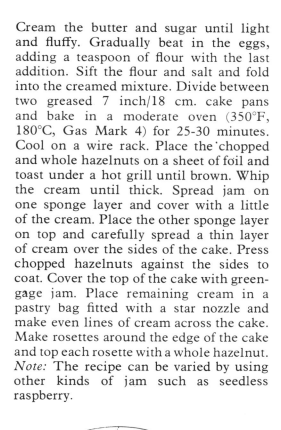

★ Swiss roll with mincemeat cream

Imperial/Metric
3 large eggs
4 oz./125 g. castor sugar
3 oz./75 g. self-raising
  flour
1 oz./25 g. butter, melted
1 tablespoon hot water
filling:
½ pint/3 dl. double cream
8 oz./225 g. mincemeat
icing sugar

American
3 large eggs
½ cup granulated sugar
¾ cup all-purpose flour
1 teaspoon baking powder
2 tablespoons melted
  butter
1 tablespoon hot water
filling:
1¼ cups whipping cream
1 cup mincemeat
confectioner's sugar

Line a sheet cake pan 9 inches/23 cm. by 14 inches/35 cm. with well greased waxed paper. Put the eggs and sugar into a bowl and beat hard until thick. Sift the flour and fold in with a metal spoon, then fold in the butter and hot water. Pour mixture into the prepared pan and bake near the top of a hot oven (425°F, 220°C, Gas Mark 7) for 10 minutes. Sprinkle a sheet of waxed paper with confectioners' sugar. When the roll is ready turn out onto the sugar and remove the paper. Put a clean sheet of waxed paper on top of the cake and roll up. Let stand until cool. To make the filling whip the cream and mix gently with the mincemeat so the cream still holds its shape. Carefully unroll the cake and spread the filling over it. Roll up and chill for 1 hour before serving. Dust with confectioners' sugar. Serves 8.

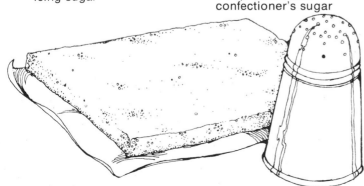

75

 # Decorated ice cream dessert

Imperial/Metric
¼ pint/1½ dl. double cream
2 tablespoons rum
few orange segments
17 fl. oz./½ litre pack Rum
  and Raisin ice cream
16 ratafia biscuits
small strip angelica

American
½ cup whipping cream
2 tablespoons rum
few orange segments
1 pint Rum Raisin
  ice cream
16 small almond macaroons
small strip angelica

Whip the cream with the rum until stiff enough to force through a pastry bag. Place in a pastry bag with a small rose nozzle. Have ready a few orange segments or other seasonal fruit to decorate. Chill a flat glass serving dish, turn out the ice cream on to the plate and quickly decorate with whipped cream rosettes round the top and at both ends. Garnish with small almond macaroons, fruit and leaves of angelica. Serve at once.

Grapefruit Alaska

Imperial/Metric
2 fresh grapefruit
2 tablespoons sweet sherry
3 egg whites
3 oz./75 g. castor sugar
½ teaspoon vanilla essence
4 scoops vanilla ice cream

American
2 fresh grapefruit
2 tablespoons sweet sherry
3 egg whites
⅓ cup granulated sugar
½ teaspoon vanilla extract
4 scoops vanilla ice cream

Cut the grapefruit in half, separate the segments and sprinkle with the sherry. Beat the egg whites until soft peaks form. Gradually add the sugar, beating until very stiff peaks form. Add the vanilla extract. At serving time, top each grapefruit half with a scoop of ice cream. Cover the ice cream with the meringue, sealing the ice cream with the meringue to the edge of the grapefruit. Place on a baking sheet in a very hot oven (475°F, 240°C, Gas Mark 9) for 3 minutes. Serve immediately.

Note: Cut a very thin slice of peel off the bottom of each grapefruit to ensure that it rests firmly on the baking sheet.

Frozen date and nut pie

Imperial/Metric
8 digestive biscuits
1½ oz./40 g. butter
1 tablespoons castor sugar
1 pint/generous ½ litre vanilla ice cream
4 oz./125 g. chopped dates
3 fl. oz./75 ml. water
1 tablespoon sugar
2 teaspoons lemon juice
¼ pint/1½ dl. double cream
2 tablespoons castor sugar
½ teaspoon vanilla essence
1 oz./25 g. chopped walnuts

American
12 Graham crackers
3 tablespoons melted butter
1 tablespoon granulated sugar
2½ cups vanilla ice cream
⅔ cup chopped dates
⅓ cup water
1 tablespoon granulated sugar
2 teaspoons lemon juice
½ cup whipping cream
2 tablespoons granulated sugar
½ teaspoon vanilla extract
¼ cup chopped walnuts

Crush the Graham crackers. Melt the butter and stir into the crumbs with the sugar. Press into an 8 inch/20 cm. pie pan and bake in a moderate oven (350°F, 180°C, Gas Mark 4) for 5 minutes. Cool. Stir the ice cream to soften and spoon into the cracker crust. Place in the freezer. Combine the dates, water and sugar in a small saucepan. Cover and cook for 5 minutes or until soft. Stir in the lemon juice and let cool. Spread half the date mixture over the ice cream. Beat the cream lightly: fold in the sugar, vanilla extract, chopped walnuts and remaining date mixture. Spread over the date mixture in the cracker crust. Freeze. Serves 6-8.

Orange sundaes flambés

Imperial/Metric
3 large oranges
1 oz./25 g. dates, chopped
4 fl. oz./125 ml. orange juice
1 oz./25 g. flaked almonds, toasted
2 tablespoons Cointreau
2 tablespoons brandy
8 scoops vanilla ice cream

American
3 large oranges
¼ cup chopped dates
½ cup orange juice
¼ cup toasted flaked almonds
2 tablespoons Cointreau
2 tablespoons brandy
8 scoops vanilla ice cream

Peel the oranges, removing all the white pith. Dice the orange flesh and combine with the chopped dates and orange juice. Allow to stand for 1 hour. At serving time, pile up the scoops of ice cream in a serving-dish. Pour the orange and date sauce into a chafing dish and heat until slightly thickened. Stir in the toasted almonds. Warm the Cointreau and brandy. Pour over the sauce and ignite. Ladle the flaming orange sauce over the ice cream.

Hostess specials

Toiling over elaborate desserts may not be your forte, but some delightful home-made delicacies need no cooking. Making mincemeat is merely an assembly task, and even the tiresome chore of mincing the fruit can be omitted. Chop, grate, squeeze and stir all together; then it is ready to put into jars. *Petits fours* have always been expensive, and some are rather elaborate confections. Using prepared almond paste, these exotic little numbers are quick to make and cost far less than those bought from a continental *patisserie*.

As for glacé fruits, I have always wondered why my guests regard these with awe. Anyone who can boil sugar and water and is deft enough not to burn her fingers with the caramel can make them in a few minutes. But the paper candy cups do add a professional touch.

Glacé fruits

Imperial/Metric
1 seedless satsuma or
  clementine
3 oz./75 g. sugar
3 tablespoons water
12 black grapes

American
1 seedless satsuma or
  clementine
$\frac{1}{3}$ cup granulated sugar
3 tablespoons water
12 Tokay grapes

Peel the clementine and divide into segments, removing as much white pith as possible. Place the sugar and water in a small saucepan and bring slowly to the boil making sure that the sugar dissolves before the mixture boils. Once sugar has dissolved do not stir. Boil until syrup just begins to turn pale straw colour. Immediately drop pieces of fruit one at a time into the syrup, removing with two skewers on to a board. Spoon any remaining syrup over the fruit before it sets. Place in paper candy cups before completely cold and set to avoid them sticking to the board.

Marrons glacés

Imperial/Metric
2 lbs./1 kg. large chestnuts
1 lb./450 g. sugar
½ pint/3 dl. water
pinch cream of tartar
2 teaspoons vanilla essence
second syrup:
1 lb./450 g. sugar
¼ pint/1½ dl. water
1 teaspoon vanilla essence

American
2 lb. large chestnuts
2 cups granulated sugar
1¼ cups water
pinch cream of tartar
2 teaspoons vanilla extract
second syrup:
2 cups sugar
generous ½ cup water
1 teaspoon vanilla extract

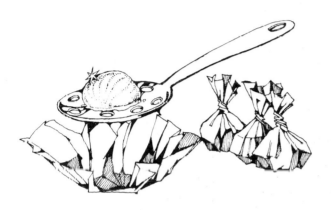

Slit the shells and boil the chestnuts for 5 minutes only. Skin, cook until tender in sufficient water to cover, flavored with the vanilla extract. Make a syrup with the sugar, water and cream of tartar. Boil to the thread stage (225°F, 119°C). Add the chestnuts and boil for 1 minute. Remove from the heat, let chestnuts soak for 24 hours, drain. Make the second syrup with the sugar, water and vanilla extract. Boil to the firm ball stage (250°F, 126°C). Add the chestnuts, coat well with the syrup, remove with a slotted spoon and space out to dry on a sheet of foil. If you wish, spoon a little extra syrup over each one. Wrap individually in foil.
Note: The remaining syrups need not be wasted. Combine them, heat slowly and re-dissolve, add a small lump of butter and 2 tablespoons rum. Peel and slice 4 bananas lengthwise, arrange in a buttered shallow ovenproof dish, pour the rum syrup over them and bake in a hot oven (425°F, 220°C, Gas Mark 7) for 10 minutes.

French petits fours

Imperial/Metric
4 oz./125 g. fresh or
  boxed dates
8 oz./225 g. marzipan
red and green food
  colourings
4 oz./125 g. plain
  chocolate

American
¾ cup whole dates
8 oz. almond paste
  (marzipan)
red and green food
  colorings
4 oz. bitter chocolate

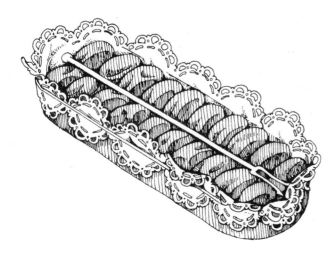

Stone the dates. Keep aside two thirds of the marzipan and use the remaining third to roll into small shapes, the same size as the date pits parts. Divide the remaining marzipan into three. Leave one third plain and color the other two portions with red and green coloring respectively by patting out the marzipan, sprinkling with a few drops of the coloring and working this in by kneading it until paste is evenly colored. Roll out all three pieces between your hands into ropes about 6 inches/15 cm. long. Press two ropes close together on a board, and place the third rope between them on top. Make sure the different colors are firmly pressed together. Melt the chocolate in a basin over a pan of hot water. Pour over the marzipan roll, spread with a palette knife and allow to set. When quite dry, pass a palette knife under the roll to loosen it and cut into ½ inch/1 cm. slices diagonally with a sharp knife. Place the stuffed dates and marzipan slices in paper candy cups.

Brandied mincemeat

Imperial/Metric
1½ lbs./¾ kg. cooking apples
8 oz /225 g. mixed
  candied peel
4 oz./125 g. blanched
  almonds
8 oz./225 g. glacé cherries
1 orange
1 lemon
1 lb./450 g. currants
1 lb./450 g. seedless
  raisins
1 lb/450 g. demerara
  sugar
1 lb./450 g. shredded suet
½ teaspoon salt
½ teaspoon mixed spice
1 teaspoon grated nutmeg
¼ pint/1½ dl. brandy

American
1½ lbs. baking apples
2 cups mixed candied peel
1 cup blanched almonds
2 cups candied cherries
1 orange
1 lemon
2½ cups currants
generous 3 cups seedless
  raisins
2 cups brown sugar
2¾ cups finely chopped suet
½ teaspoon salt
½ teaspoon mixed spice
1 teaspoon grated nutmeg
½ cup brandy

Peel, core and chop apples. Finely chop the peel, almonds, and cherries. Grate the rind of the orange and lemon, and squeeze the juice. Stir all the ingredients together until well blended. Cover, and allow to stand for 2 days. Pack into clean jars and seal as for jam. Makes approximately 7 lbs.

Note: To make a finer mincemeat, put all the dried and candied fruit through the food chopper. To make the flavor of your mincemeat even richer, small amounts of fruit liqueur and fortified wines can be used instead of part of the brandy or the fruit juice. Add a little extra sugar when using mincemeat for cooking. Keeps well for one year, and requires at least 1 month to mature, otherwise a suety flavor may predominate.

Seasonal home freezing

This is the time of the year when hearty soups, warming casseroles and similar dishes are called for to combat the cold.

Cooking a casserole in the oven becomes more economical if you double the quantity, serve one portion right away, and freeze a second portion for later use. Think of the savings in fuel and your energy.

The main event during the winter season is Christmas and if you have family and friends to stay during that time you do not want to be slaving away in the kitchen. By following the pre-Christmas preparation plan on page 83, and freezing the fare beforehand you will be able to relax and enjoy your Christmas entertaining.

Beef ragoût with corn

Imperial/Metric
1½ lb./¾ kg. chuck steak
1 tablespoon dripping or lard
2 medium onions, chopped
4 medium carrots, chopped
1 tablespoon flour
1 pint/6 fl. hot beef stock
2 teaspoons tomato purée
1 clove garlic
salt and pepper
1 bay leaf
1 tablespoon chopped parsley
4 oz./100 g. frozen sweet-corn.

American
1½ lb. chuck steak
1 tablespoon dripping or lard
2 medium onions, chopped
4 medium carrots, chopped
1 tablespoon flour
2½ cups hot beef broth
2 teaspoons tomato paste
1 clove garlic
salt and pepper
1 bay leaf
1 tablespoon chopped parsley
1 cup frozen kernel corn

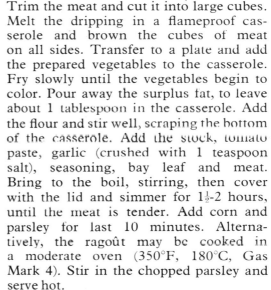

Trim the meat and cut it into large cubes. Melt the dripping in a flameproof casserole and brown the cubes of meat on all sides. Transfer to a plate and add the prepared vegetables to the casserole. Fry slowly until the vegetables begin to color. Pour away the surplus fat, to leave about 1 tablespoon in the casserole. Add the flour and stir well, scraping the bottom of the casserole. Add the stock, tomato paste, garlic (crushed with 1 teaspoon salt), seasoning, bay leaf and meat. Bring to the boil, stirring, then cover with the lid and simmer for 1½-2 hours, until the meat is tender. Add corn and parsley for last 10 minutes. Alternatively, the ragoût may be cooked in a moderate oven (350°F, 180°C, Gas Mark 4). Stir in the chopped parsley and serve hot.

To freeze: Cool, cover surface with plastic wrap, cover with the lid, and label. When frozen, remove casserole lid. (If preferred, transfer the ragoût to a plastic container, seal and label.)

To serve: Remove plastic wrap. Reheat, from the frozen state, in a moderate oven (350°F, 180°C, Gas Mark 4) for 45 minutes – 1 hour. Remove the bay leaf before serving. Serves 6.

(Certain types of casserole such as the one shown on the opposite page can be taken straight from the freezer to the oven without any danger of them cracking.)

Reorganizing ready for Christmas

At Christmas, and other times during the year, when you will be called upon to do some special catering, possibly for a large number, your freezer will be worth its weight in gold.

A certain amount of pre-planning is necessary in order to ensure that the Christmas entertaining will go off without a hitch, but it is time well spent and will leave you free to enjoy the company of your guests without being reduced to a state of nervous exhaustion.

Go through your freezer log and make a note of all the items (including blanched and non-blanched vegetables, made-up dishes, cakes, bread and muffins) which have been in the freezer for the last 9-12 months, and endeavor to plan your menus for the next few weeks with those foods in mind. Decide what you will need for Christmas in the way of made-up dishes. Look up any special recipes and start to make detailed shopping and preparation lists.

Defrosting the freezer: When the stocks in your freezer are reasonably low is the time to defrost it. (Naturally, the best time is when the freezer is completely empty, but that is a counsel of perfection.)

To defrost the freezer, switch it off, remove all the packages and, depending on how many you have, place them in the freezing compartment of the refrigerator, in insulated bags, or sacks (available from frozen-food stores) or wrap in several layers of newspaper and place them all together in a stout box. Place in the coolest spot—a garage, porch or spare bedroom. Take out the removable baskets and shelves (if yours is an upright) from the freezer and place a layer of foam plastic or an old sheet in the bottom. Allow the build-up of frost to soften, then with a plastic scraper gently scrape the frost from the inside walls and immovable shelves of the freezer. Never use a knife or other sharp instrument which would cause damage to the interior of the cabinet. It is also advisable to wear a pair of rubber gloves for this operation. When all the frost has been scraped off and has collected in the bottom, simply lift out the foam plastic or sheet and squeeze it dry. Mop up any remaining water and wipe the interior with a bicarbonate of soda solution (1 tablespoon bicarbonate of soda to 2 pints/generous litre water). Now wipe dry with a clean, dry tea towel. To hasten the defrosting, a bowl of hot water may be placed in the freezer. Close the lid, or door, switch on again and allow the inside of the cabinet to drop to the required temperature—this will take about 1 hour—before repacking the food into the freezer. See the freezer hints on page 83.

If any strong-smelling foods (Brussels sprouts and broccoli, in particular) have been stored in the freezer and you still detect an unpleasant smell in the cabinet, use the following solution to wipe out the inside: 1 tablespoon bicarbonate of soda, $\frac{1}{2}$ pint/3 dl./$1\frac{1}{4}$ cups vinegar to 8 pints/$4\frac{1}{2}$ litres/9 pints water.

If your freezer has an automatic defrosting cycle it is not necessary to empty it for the defrosting process. The defrosting cycle takes place automatically at certain periods, while the freezer is in operation, thus prohibiting the build-up of any frost. All that is necessary is for the tray of water to be emptied.

The exterior of the freezer can be kept clean and shiny by wiping it over with white furniture cream or spray-on polish. Tempting as it may be, avoid using the top of a chest freezer as a storage area. Not only will it become scratched, but it makes life difficult to have to clear the top of the freezer before you can get into it.

Freezer hints: When re-packing the food into the freezer after defrosting, remember to leave areas which are easily accessible for the Christmas stocks which you will be preparing in the coming weeks. If you intend purchasing a frozen turkey and have an upright freezer, you may need to re-arrange the shelves in order to accommodate, it, particularly if you are buying a large turkey. Leave the baskets of a chest freezer and the fast-freeze compartment empty, ready for the new arrivals.

Labelling: It is important that every package that is put into a freezer is labelled, but with the Christmas stocks it is a good idea to have a special labelling system. For example, use the same color labels for all Christmas stocks and for special party fare. Seal packages with special adhesive tape on which you can write the date and contents. A good way of keeping all the Christmas packages together, especially in a chest freezer, is to place them in one basket, batching bag or carrier bag and label accordingly. For clear and easy-to-read labels, punch-printed ones are excellent. The small Dymos which punch out the labels are not expensive to purchase, and as well as labels for freezer packages, they can also be used to make labels for kitchen storage jars. Different colored tapes are available so that you can carry out your color coding system.

Freezing ahead for the holidays

During the two weeks before Christmas start to prepare and freeze the dishes for the holiday period. Cross the dishes off your preparation list once they are in the freezer, and remember to enter them in your freezer log.

Bread sauce: This can be made and stored in the freezer in a plastic container, leaving a headspace.

Poultry stuffings: Your chosen stuffings can be prepared and stored, wrapped in freezer foil. It is not a good idea to stuff poultry before freezing. Stuffings suitable for turkey and chicken include chestnut, and parsley and thyme (forcemeat); for goose and duck, sage and onion. Fresh breadcrumbs which you will need for the above two items can have been made from left-over pieces of white bread in the preceding weeks. Freeze the breadcrumbs in a plastic container or bag sealed with a twist tie. By far the quickest way of making breadcrumbs is to place cubes of bread in the blender where they can be reduced to fine breadcrumbs at a flick of the switch. Alternatively, rub the bread through a sieve, or rub it on a grater to make the crumbs.

Sausages in pastry wraps (sausage rolls) and mince pies: This is another time-consuming job which can be got out of the way in the two weeks prior to Christmas. Make some small sausage rolls, which are ideal to serve with drinks, from either defrosted frozen puff pastry or the chilled puff pastry which is available from some supermarkets. Place them (unbaked) in a plastic container, with foil or cardboard dividers to enable you to remove only as many as you may require at a time. Place the frozen rolls straight on a baking sheet, brush with beaten egg and bake in a hot oven (425°F, 220°C, Gas Mark 7) for 15-20 minutes. If you wish, a couple of slits may be made in the top of each sausage roll after they have been glazed.

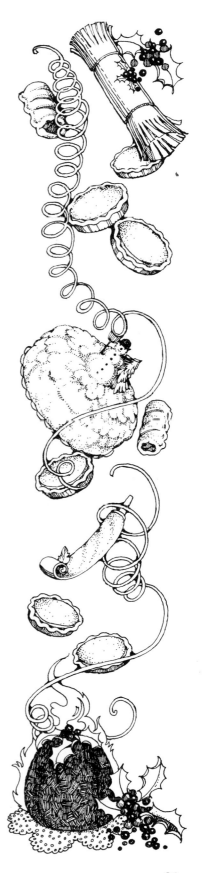

Mince tarts are nicest made with an enriched short pastry – 8 oz./ 225 g./2 cups plain flour, 5 oz./150 g./generous ½ cup butter, 1 egg yolk and 1 tablespoon sugar dissolved in 2 teaspoons water – particularly if you intend to serve sausage rolls made with puff pastry. Again, store the mince tarts unbaked, to enable you to bake them as required in a moderately hot oven (400°F, 200°C, Gas Mark 6) for 25-30 minutes. 8 oz. flour etc. will make 8-12 mince tarts, depending on the size. When preparing mince tarts for the freezer, open freeze them in the patty tins, then remove from the tins and pack. Serve with a sprinkling of confectioners' sugar, and with brandy or Cumberland butter.

Brandy butter: This is delicious served with mince tarts and the Christmas pudding. Beat together 6 oz./175 g./¾ cup unsalted butter and 8 oz./225 g./2 cups sieved confectioners' sugar until light and creamy. Beat in brandy to taste – do not use your best brandy for this, the cheaper variety will do – and pack the mixture in plastic containers. Seal and label. A nice touch when serving the brandy butter is to spike and label. A nice touch when serving the brandy butter is to spike the surface with slivered almonds. With the freezer as your friend and ally, it is no trouble to add these little extras when entertaining.

Cumberland butter: Carefully melt 8 oz./225 g./1 cup unsalted butter over a low heat without allowing it to froth or brown. Place 1lb./450 g./ 2 cups soft brown sugar and a pinch of nutmeg in a bowl. Pour in 3 tablespoons rum and mix well. Gradually add the melted butter, beating the mixture with a wooden spoon until it begins to harden. Pack in plastic containers, seal, label and store in the freezer until required.

Freezing citrus fruits

These may be frozen in various ways, depending on the time you have available and how you intend to use the frozen fruit. For example, whole Seville oranges may be frozen for marmalade making. Orange and grapefruit segments may be frozen in a sugar syrup and used in a fruit cocktail or salad; for decorating cheesecakes and gâteaux or for adding to fruit cups. The citrus fruit juice may be frozen in ice cube trays and the cubes packed in a plastic bag – ideal for use in drinks and for recipes which call for fresh orange, lemon or grapefruit juice. The grated rind may be mixed with sugar, stored in plastic containers and used in baking recipes.

Syrup pack: For citrus fruits, a 40% syrup, i.e. 11 oz./300 g./generous 1¼ cups granulated sugar to 1 pint/6 dl/2½ cups water is ideal as it helps to counteract any sharpness in the fruit without making it too sweet for future use. To make the syrup, place the sugar and water in a pan over low heat. Slowly bring to the boil and allow the sugar to dissolve completely, then boil for 2-3 minutes. Cool, then chill overnight in the refrigerator before using. Peel the fruit, divide into segments, removing the seeds and membranes. Place the prepared fruit in plastic containers and pour over sufficient syrup just to cover the fruit. Leave a ½ inch/1 cm. headspace, and as fruit tends to rise in a syrup pack, place a piece of crumpled foil in the top of the container before sealing and labelling. The foil will freeze into the syrup, but can be easily removed on defrosting.

Freezing citrus fruits whole: Wash, dry and pack the fruit in plastic bags. Label and seal with a twist tie. While the fruit is frozen it is easy to grate the rind from grapefruit, lemons and oranges for use in baking recipes.

Concentrated soups

Soups are great for entertaining hungry guests, feeding a growing family and providing a quick and nourishing lunch. Storing the basis for different soups, in concentrated form, in the freezer will enable you to produce a good soup with the addition of milk, milk and water, or milk and cream. It is also economical on freezer storage space—a consideration, particularly at Christmas time.

A blender is an asset in making soups, preventing wastage of ingredients, but it is possible to make them by pressing the vegetables through a sieve, or by using a Mouli soup mill. This removes traces of coarse fibres, tomato seeds, etc.

To make the basis for a vegetable soup: Melt 2 oz./50 g./2 tablespoons of butter in a frying pan and sauté 1 lb./450 g. chopped vegetables (a mixture of onion, carrots, leeks and celery) until softened, but not browned. Add ½ pint/3 dl./1½ cups stock and simmer over a moderate heat until the vegetables are cooked. Add seasoning and a pinch of herbs, if you wish. Allow the mixture to cool slightly before blending or sieving. Cool, then pack the purée in plastic containers, leaving a headspace. Seal and label.

To serve the soup, gently reheat the purée in a pan, stirring to avoid sticking. Add an equal amount of liquid—milk, or milk and water—bring just to the boil and check the seasoning. Cream and chopped parsley may be stirred in just before serving the soup.

Broad beans, cauliflower florets, potatoes, celery, leeks, mushrooms and carrots can all be used as a soup basis. Avocado pears also make a good soup, particularly overripe ones which are not suitable to serve as a starter. The method for avocado soup is slightly different. Peel the avocados, halve and remove the stones. Mash to a purée (if the avocados are soft they can be masked in a bowl with a fork) and add seasoning, and lemon juice to prevent discoloration. Freeze in plastic containers. To make the soup, reheat the purée gently, stirring to avoid sticking, and add sufficient milk and chicken stock to make the required consistency. Serve with a swirl of cream in each portion. Avocado soup can also be served chilled. This way it makes a good starter, particularly if you are serving hot second and third courses. Most vegetable soups, in fact, are delicious served chilled.

Purées of root vegetables: Now that root vegetables are in season it makes good sense to freeze them for future use. A purée takes far less space in the freezer than prepared, blanched vegetables. Prepare the vegetables (young parsnips and turnips, carrots) according to type and cook in boiling, salted water until tender. Drain well and mash or blend to a purée, adding more seasoning, if liked. Ground black pepper goes well with parsnips, turnips and carrots. Alternatively, try a sprinkling of ground nutmeg. Sautéed chopped onion blended to a purée is a useful standby in the freezer for use in stuffings. Jerusalem artichokes, which are available at this time of the year, may also be prepared as parsnips etc. and stored as a purée. When storing purées, remember to leave a small headspace in the container. To serve the vegetables, transfer to a pan and reheat over a low heat, with a piece of butter, stirring to prevent sticking. Vegetable purées go well with roast meats, poultry and game. They may also be served with casseroles, but in order to give a contrast of textures to the meal do not serve creamed potatoes as well. Boiled or jacket potatoes would be better in this case.

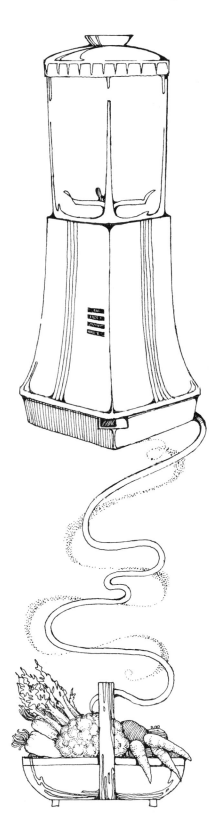

How to freeze nuts

Shelled almonds, walnuts, hazelnuts, brazils, peanuts and cashews all freeze well and you will be surprised at the good results. However, it is better to add salt on defrosting rather than freeze them with the salt added. They may be frozen whole, chopped or slivered for use in teabreads, cakes and scones. Another method is to sauté them in heated butter with a little oil added to prevent the butter from burning. Drain on absorbent paper and allow to cool before packing and sealing in plastic containers. The different varieties can be frozen in separate containers or frozen together as mixed nuts. For salted nuts, toss the defrosted nuts in salt, or sprinkle generously with sea salt.

Coffee and nut ice cream

Imperial/Metric
2 eggs
4 tablespoons sieved icing sugar
2 tablespoons coffee essence
¼ pint/1½ dl. double cream
2 oz./50 g. walnuts or hazelnuts, coarsely chopped

American
2 eggs
5 tablespoons sifted confectioners' sugar
3 tablespoons strong black coffee
⅔ cup heavy cream
1 cup coarsely chopped walnuts or hazelnuts

Separate the eggs and whisk the whites until stiff. Fold in the sieved confectioners' sugar. Whip the egg yolks and coffee essence together. Combine the two mixtures, beating gently. Whip the cream until slightly thickened, then fold into the mixture together with the chopped nuts. Spoon the mixture into freezing trays, or a plastic container.

To freeze: Seal, label and place in the freezer. This ice cream does not need any further beating.

To serve: Allow to soften slightly before scooping out of the container. Serve sprinkled with a few extra chopped nuts and chocolate sauce, if you wish.

Date and walnut teabread

Imperial/Metric
12 oz./350 g. self-raising flour
¼ teaspoon mixed spices
4 oz./100 g. butter or margarine
2 oz./50 g. castor sugar
2 oz./50 g. walnuts, chopped
2 oz./50 g. dates, chopped
1 egg
¼ pint/1½ dl. milk
1 tablespoon black treacle

American
3 cups all-purpose flour sifted with 3 teaspoons baking powder
¼ teaspoon mixed spice
½ cup butter or margarine
¼ cup granulated sugar
½ cup chopped walnuts
¼ cup chopped dates
1 egg
⅔ cup milk
1 tablespoon molasses

Sift the flour and mixed spices into a bowl. Rub in the butter until the mixture resembles fine breadcrumbs. Stir in the sugar, walnuts and dates. Lightly beat the egg and milk together, and add to the dry ingredients with the molasses. Beat the mixture thoroughly with a wooden spoon until well mixed. Spoon into a 2 lb./1 kg. loaf pan, previously lined at the base with waxed paper and brushed with melted fat. Bake in a moderately hot oven (350°F, 180°C, Gas Mark 4) for 1-1¼ hours, until nicely risen and firm to the touch. Leave in the pan for a few minutes, then turn out and cool on a wire rack.

To freeze: Wrap in freezer foil, or place in a plastic bag. Seal and label.

To serve: Remove the wrapping and thaw at room temperature for about 1 hour. Serve in slices spread with butter.

Using left-over turkey

There are many ways of using up the cooked turkey meat when you feel you have had enough served cold with sauces, pickles and relishes. The darker meat from the legs and wings is ideal for use in the following recipes. Cooked turkey meat may also be turned into a curry, added to a white sauce and used as a savory filling for pies, pancakes or vol-au-vents; a pilaff or risotto, a savory mousse, or minced and perhaps mixed with minced ham to make a turkey and ham loaf or patties. Prepare a selection of these cooked dishes and store them in the freezer for future use. Finally, to ensure that all the turkey is utilized, make stock for the freezer from the carcass. When cold, freeze some in plastic containers (remember to leave a headspace) and some as frozen cubes – the cubes of concentrated stock will be ideal for adding to, and enriching, sauces and poultry casseroles.

★ Turkey and noodle casserole

Imperial/Metric
3 oz./75 g. butter
about 1 oz./25 g. flour
1 pint/6 dl. turkey stock
½ pint/3 dl. single cream
6 tablespoons dry white wine
3 oz./75 g. grated Parmesan cheese
12 oz./350 g. mushrooms, sliced
8 oz./225 g. noodles
1½-2 lb./¾-1 kg. cooked turkey meat, chopped
salt and pepper

American
6 tablespoons butter
5 tablespoons flour
2½ cups turkey stock
1¼ cups coffee cream
½ cup dry white wine
¾ cup grated Parmesan cheese
3 cups sliced mushrooms
½ lb. noodles
3-4 cups chopped cooked turkey meat
salt and pepper

Melt 1 oz./25 g./2 tablespoons of the butter in a pan and stir in the flour. Cook for 2-3 minutes, stirring, to prevent the flour from becoming brown. Gradually stir in the stock. Bring to the boil over a moderate heat, stirring until thickened. Stir in the cream and wine and reheat, but do not allow to boil. Stir in 2 oz./50 g./ ½ cup of the cheese. Melt the remaining butter in a frying pan and sauté the mushrooms until lightly browned. Cook the noodles in a pan of boiling, salted water until just tender. Drain well.

In a large casserole (or, if more convenient, use shaped foil dishes), place two-thirds of the sauce, the mushrooms, noodles and turkey, in layers. Add salt and pepper to taste and top with the remaining sauce. Sprinkle over the reserved grated cheese. Cool.

To freeze: Cover and label.

To serve: Reheat, from the frozen state, in a moderately hot oven (375°F, 190°C, Gas Mark 5) for 1 hour for a large casserole, or for about 30 minutes for smaller portions. If you wish, a little more grated cheese may be sprinkled on the top before reheating. Serves 4-6.

Turkey and artichoke savory

Imperial/Metric
1 oz./25 g. butter
4 oz./100 g. mushrooms, sliced
½ oz./15 g. flour
¼ pint/1½ dl. turkey stock
2 tablespoons sherry
pinch dried rosemary
salt and pepper
½ teaspoon paprika pepper
1 lb./450 g. cooked turkey meat, chopped
1 lb./450 g. can artichoke hearts, drained

American
2 tablespoons butter
1 cup sliced mushrooms
2 tablespoons all purpose flour
⅔ cup turkey stock
3 tablespoons sherry
dash dried rosemary
salt and pepper
½ teaspoon paprika
2 cups chopped cooked turkey meat
1 lb. can artichoke hearts, drained

Melt the butter in a pan and sauté the mushrooms until lightly browned. Sprinkle in the flour and cook for a further 1-2 minutes, stirring. Gradually add the stock and sherry, stirring. Add the rosemary and seasoning. Place the turkey and drained artichoke hearts in a casserole, or shaped foil container, and pour over the mushroom mixture. Cool.

To freeze: Cover and label.

To serve: Reheat, from the frozen state, in a moderately hot oven (375°F, 190°C, Gas Mark 5) for about 30 minutes, adding a little extra stock if necessary.

Turkey with glazed chicory

Imperial/Metric
1 lb./450 g. chicory, trimmed
1 lb./450 g. cooked turkey, chopped
1 tablespoon vinegar
8 oz./227 g. can tomatoes
1 oz./25 g. butter
1 oz./25 g. demerara sugar
½ teaspoon dried oregano
salt and pepper

American
1 lb. Belgian endive, trimmed
1 lb. cooked turkey, chopped
1 tablespoon vinegar
1 cup canned tomatoes
2 tablespoons butter
2 tablespoons brown sugar
½ teaspoon dried oregano
salt and pepper

Cook the endive heads in boiling salted water until just tender but not soft, and add the vinegar to avoid discoloration. Drain, mix with the turkey, place in an ovenproof serving dish. Heat the tomatoes with the butter, sugar, herbs and seasoning to taste and simmer for 3 minutes. Sieve and pour over the endive, to coat well. Cool.

To freeze: Cover and label.

To serve: Reheat from the frozen state, in a moderately hot oven (375°F, 190°C, Gas Mark 5) for about 30 minutes.

Winter party plan —
Making Christmas a pleasure

Every hostess cooks for compliments at Christmas, but not necessarily because hers are the best baked mince tarts or the most evenly browned turkey. Guests will welcome the originality of your catering if you offer a choice of these more unusual dishes and drinks.

Christmas Eve: When friends or relatives drop in on Christmas Eve, serve Cranberry rosé or Gourmet egg flip with hot or cold hors d'oeuvre.

☆ Cranberry rosé

Imperial/Metric
1 lb./450 g. cranberries
1½ pints/scant 1 litre water
10 oz./275 g. castor sugar
½ teaspoon salt
¼ pint/1½ dl. orange juice
2 fl. oz./50 ml. lemon juice
1¾ pints/1 litre rosé wine

American
1 lb. cranberries
4 cups water
1¼ cups granulated sugar
½ teaspoon salt
½ cup orange juice
¼ cup lemon juice
1 litre rosé wine

Cook the cranberries in the water until tender. Strain and add the sugar and salt to the juice. Bring to the boil, stirring until the sugar is dissolved. Add the fruit juices. Chill. Just before serving add the rosé wine.

Gourmet's egg flip: For each serving beat one egg yolk with a tablespoon of sugar, 2 fl. oz./50 ml. heavy cream and 2 fl. oz./50 ml. rum, whisky or brandy. Fold in one stiffly beaten egg white and a few grains of salt. Sprinkle with cinnamon or nutmeg.

Hors d'oeuvre: Spear on cocktail sticks:
—avocado cubes dipped in lemon juice
—pineapple pieces and Camembert cheese cubes
—melon or cucumber fingers wrapped in paper-thin roast beef slices
—prawns dipped in curried mayonnaise
—apple wedges dipped in lemon juice with blue cheese cubes
—cheese cubes with pickled onions rolled in toasted breadcrumbs
—banana fingers dipped in lemon juice and rolled in chopped nuts

Spreads for savory biscuits:
—sardines mashed with lemon juice and sprinkled with paprika
—crumbled blue cheese on thin tomato slices spread with mayonnaise
—cream cheese sprinkled with chopped nuts
—chopped prawns and chicken livers garnished with capers
—Camembert cheese and finely chopped dill pickle
—chopped prawns mixed with mayonnaise and topped with pineapple pieces
—tuna fish mashed with cream cheese and lemon juice
—minced ham and French mustard

Unusual hot hors d'oeuvre:
—spread toast triangles with grated Cheddar cheese mixed with mayonnaise. Sprinkle with paprika and grill until bubbly and brown.
—heat contents of a small can of drained cocktail sausages in two tablespoons prepared mustard mixed with 4 tablespoons red currant jelly. Spear on cocktail sticks when hot
—spoon creamed chicken into small profiteroles and heat in a moderately hot oven (400°F, 200°C, Gas Mark 6) for 10 minutes

—add flaked crabmeat and sweet corn to cheese sauce and spoon into tiny vol-au-vent cases. Heat in a moderately hot oven (400°F, 200°C, Gas Mark 6) for 10 minutes or until heated through

—spread tuna fish mixed with mayonnaise and finely chopped celery on thinly sliced buttered bread. Roll up and slice into pinwheels. Chill, brush lightly with melted butter and grill until nicely browned

—marinate chicken livers for one hour in soy sauce with a pinch of ginger and curry powder. Drain, wrap in bacon and thread on skewers. Grill until the bacon is cooked

Christmas dinner: For a light start, serve consommé with a flair. Start with canned consommé, dilute with water and add one of the following:

—a tablespoon of medium dry sherry or port

—crumbled cooked bacon and a pinch of curry powder

—chopped prawns and toasted almonds

—grated cucumber and a few drops of lime juice

—finely shredded carrots

—garnish with slices of avocado

—condensed tomato soup and a pinch of nutmeg

With the roast turkey: Serve Cranberry orange sauce or Port wine jelly.
Cranberry orange sauce: Cook 1 lb./450 g. cranberries with 1 lb./450 g. sugar and $\frac{1}{2}$ pint/3 dl. orange juice until the cranberry skins burst. Press through a sieve. Chill in the refrigerator until firm.
Port wine jelly: Dissolve 1 lb./450 g. sugar in $\frac{3}{4}$ pint/4 dl. port wine over gentle heat. Stir in 6 fl. oz./170 ml. commercial pectin. Pour into a jelly mold and chill until firm. Unmold on a glass dish.

Turkey stuffings: Try an original touch this year:

—substitute cooked long grain rice for the breadcrumbs in your usual stuffing recipe

—add dried apricots to bread or rice stuffing. (Soak the apricots in water, then chop finely)

—sauté sliced mushrooms in butter and add to bread stuffing

—add crumbled cooked bacon to bread stuffing

—add Madeira, sherry or apple brandy to chestnut stuffing

For an easy and light Christmas Day supper: Serve cold sliced turkey, Snow frosted ham, which can be made the day before, celery sticks stuffed with cheese, and buttered rolls. Roll left-over turkey stuffing in foil, refrigerate, then slice and serve cold. Take Frozen Christmas pie out of the freezer 15 minutes before serving.

Snow frosted ham: Blend cream cheese with sour cream until spreading consistency. Beat in horseradish, celery salt and black pepper to taste. Spread evenly over a cooked ham. Garnish with whole fresh cranberries and gherkin slices. Sprinkle with coarse salt. Refrigerate until required.

Frozen Christmas pie: Blend $\frac{1}{4}$ pint/$1\frac{1}{2}$ dl. cranberry sauce with one 8 oz./225 g. can drained pineapple pieces. Stir into 1 pint/generous $\frac{1}{2}$ litre vanilla ice cream. Spoon into a prepared Graham cracker crumb crust. Sprinkle with chopped nuts. Freeze.

Desserts

Offer a dessert not quite so rich as well as the traditional Christmas pudding. Try flaming mincemeat over ice cream—heat prepared mincemeat with a little orange juice and brown sugar. Warm a little rum, set alight and pour over the hot mincemeat sauce. Ladle over ice cream and garnish with toasted almonds.

For an easy freezer dessert, add mincemeat to lightly whipped heavy cream, and alternate layers of plain cookies and the mincemeat cream in a round bowl. Freeze until required, lift out of the bowl, cover with lightly whipped heavy cream sweetened with a little sugar. Garnish with holly wreaths made of glacé cherries and angelica.

For the children, make snowballs by rolling ice cream in coconut. Freeze until required and serve with hot chocolate sauce.

Fruit cake: Instead of icing your Christmas cake, glaze it immediately after baking with one of the following:

—corn syrup glaze—combine equal amounts of corn syrup and water. Simmer for a few minutes. Brush over the warm fruit cake. Decorate with candied fruit and nuts. Brush the glaze over the fruits. Return to the oven for 10 minutes.

—jelly glaze—brush warm fruit cake with melted red currant jelly or any other favorite jelly. Decorate with candied fruit and nuts. Return to the oven for 20 minutes.

—honey glaze—brush warm honey over the warm fruit cake. Decorate with candied fruits and nuts. Brush again with warm honey.

INDEX